10.25
RCa
A#1568

THE ART OF COARSE SAILING

by Michael Green

ILLUSTRATED BY JOHN JENSEN

THE ART OF

Coarse Sailing

HUTCHINSON OF LONDON

HUTCHINSON & CO. (*Publishers*) LTD
178–202 Great Portland Street, London, W.1

London Melbourne Sydney
Auckland Bombay Toronto
Johannesburg New York

First published May 1962
Second impression May 1962
Third impression November 1962
Fourth impression February 1963

This book has been set in Baskerville type face. It has
been printed in Great Britain by The Anchor Press,
Ltd., in Tiptree, Essex, on Antique Wove paper.

Foreword

THE only reason I am writing a Foreword is because a friend said that the Foreword was the funniest part of my previous book, *The Art of Coarse Rugby*. This rather hurt me, because I didn't write the Foreword—it was written by Spike Hughes. I'm taking no chance of a similar mistake this time.

My real purpose, however, is simply to thank everyone I have ever sailed with for so kindly falling in the water, sinking boats, crashing into bridges and generally helping to provide material. I should also like to thank the many strangers who have unwittingly helped, especially the honeymoon couple at Yarmouth. And, of course, Mrs. Kay Eldridge, who kindly typed the manuscript (don't worry, dear, the cheque's in the post).

Good heavens, even *my agent* chipped in with a yarn (mind you, I think he got it from Richard Gordon and I couldn't use it because he wanted 10 per cent for it). But it just shows you how kind everyone has been.

A small part of the material used in the book appeared in *The Observer* in my article 'Captains Courageous'. I have thirty or forty back-numbers for sale at five shillings each if anyone would care to write, enclosing a woollen sock.

Ealing, Acton Town Station, The
Three Pigeons, Somerleyton Swing
Bridge and Fred's Café, 1962

One

EVERY year I swear I won't spend my holiday sailing again. Considering I say this annually, it's surprising how much sailing I've managed to do. Each time I return bruised, battered and suffering from incipient scurvy, with a great dent worn in my buttocks, and I say, 'That was terrific fun, but next year I'm going to do something restful.' And somehow twelve months later I'm banging the same dent in the same place with the edge of a cockpit combing or crawling on hands and knees in some stinking bilge.

Not that much of my sailing has been particularly glamorous. I suppose most of it would qualify for the description Coarse Sailing. For those unfamiliar with Coarse sport I must refer to my definition of Coarse Rugby—a game played by fewer than fifteen a side, at least half of whom should be totally unfit. It is easier to define a Coarse Sailor than Coarse Sailing, and I think the following definition sums him up pretty well:

One who in a crisis forgets nautical language and shouts, 'For God's sake turn left.'

It's only your true-blue salt who can remember the *Manual of Seamanship* when charging into the side of a chain-ferry.

Here is an example of what I mean. I used to sail with an awfully knowledgeable chap who owned a two-berth sloop which he kept on the Hamble. Although he was most meticulous about using the correct terms ('I don't like the look of those baggy-wrinkles,' he used to say wisely), he wasn't much good really. He is the only man I know who actually ran into the Isle of Wight while trying to reach France (admittedly there was a slight fog at the time).

One day I was at the helm and our course took us slap into

7

an oil tanker. As it was his boat, I asked him for suggestions. All I wanted was something simple, like 'Oh, go round the back of her.' Instead I received a stream of the most appalling gibberish; things like 'Luff up and leave her bearing Green-four-oh.' I asked his pardon politely and he began to panic and ramble on about luffs and bearings and baggy-wrinkles and lord knows what. When a collision was nearly inevitable I shoved my face against his and asked bluntly whether he meant left or right. He never forgave me.

Another example of Coarse Sailing, a classic one, was our crossing of the Zuyder Zee, or Islemeer, that large hole in the middle of Holland which they are now, alas, filling in. When we started off from an inland Dutch boatyard we had forgotten that the Zuyder Zee was as wide as the English Channel in places, and we took no compass. A mile out of Staveren it was plain we should have to navigate. Our first wheeze was to follow the railway ferry, but he went too fast and would not slow down, although we asked him very politely. Then we hit on the idea of sticking two nails in the deck and keeping the sun's shadow constant in relation to them.

Believe it or not, but it worked. Theoretically, of course, you will sail in a circle, but we allowed for that and to our surprise hit the opposite shore not more than four or five miles from where we were aiming. After making that landfall we knew the feeling Columbus must have had when the look-out called, 'I say, Skipper, I think that's America just ahead.' (Columbus, of course, said, 'No, it's India.')

The true home of all Coarse Sailors is the Norfolk Broads. By Broads in this connection I really mean the system of narrow rivers that links the Broads proper, which are, of course, shallow lakes of differing sizes, delightfully pretty but dull from a Coarse Sailing point of view, since they offer few hazards.

It is fashionable among yachtsmen to sneer at the Broads and refer to sailing there as ditch-crawling. There is some truth in the saying that while yachting is mucking around in boats, sailing on the Broads is boating around in muck. But tacking a thirty-foot sloop against wind and tide up a narrow river crowded with other traffic can tax one's skill more than whistling across Chichester Harbour with the wind on the beam.

That's the beauty of the Broads. They compress an awful lot into a short time. You will do more tacking in one hour there than in a week of sea-sailing.

There are other hazards which do not affect the salt-water sailor, and I speak as one who has put his boom through the window of a grocer's shop and caught his gaff on an electricity cable. You don't have *those* hazards in the Channel.

The Broads have certainly provided me with as much excitement as I or my friends have found sailing elsewhere. Over the years our little flotilla has suffered every known marine disaster. These include not only the more common upsets, such as going aground, being rammed, falling overboard and so forth, but others more exotic, such as Insanity of Ship's Master, Sinking, Death of Passenger, Burial at Sea, Restraint by Forces of Law and Explosion of Vessel, most of which are described in the following chapters. We have also been under fire on the Broads, when some fool let off a duck-gun as we passed along the River Bure and the pellets thudded into the mainsail. The ducks remained quite undisturbed while we dived for shelter. Later the lunatic who fired said he mistook us for a rare bird in the dusk.

The point about incidents like this is that they satisfy the inner craving of every Englishman worth his salt to feel himself a sailor, an ocean adventurer, a real member of the race which settled half the globe and even penetrated into parts of Wales. It's that which makes people sail, whether on the sea, the Broads or the Thames. That is why they put up with the appalling discomforts of sailing when they might be doing something more sensible, such as going on a cricket tour.

I personally cherish a belief that somewhere in the family was an old sea-dog. I feel sure that on the maternal side, which is West Country, was once a Brixham skipper named Jem Green (the fact that his name would not have been Green is nothing to do with it).

Jem was tough but lovable, the sort of sea-dog who was always writing things like this in the log:

March 1: Weather v. stormy. Water v. low. Crew v. mutinous. Food bad. Two hands dead of French disease.

March 2: Weather worse. French disease rampant. Scurvy v. bad. Hanged two hands. MEM: Sextant is faulty, or am sailing up Ludgate Hill.

March 3: Accidentally shot albatross in morning. Hurricane immediately blew up.

One also likes to feel that old Jem was a bit of a moralist in the best Victorian tradition, and the author of a poem running something like this:

Jem Green's Ode

When the gale-force winds of adversity
Cause a sailor to take in a reef,
Then he ties the cringle of living clean
To the boom of an honest belief.

For you cannot luff through life, my boy,
When the wind of ill-fortune blows.
So make firm your grip on the tiller of hope
And Heavenwards swing your bows.

Then perchance it will softly come o'er you
That the main is awaiting ahead.
And life will abound in its glory
When the green on the starboard shows red.*

There is a great deal of old Jem Green in all of us, or so we like to think.

As there was in the little man I met in Bosham harbour, sitting smoking in a clinker-built dinghy and writing in a notebook.

It turned out that he was keeping a log of his holiday. Three days previously he had hired the dinghy from Itchenor, about two miles away, and had painstakingly sailed round the corner to Bosham. Since then, he explained, the wind had been too strong to set forth again.

* Whatever that means.

He showed me his log. It went something like this:

August 3: Sailed 09.00 hours. Wind force 2. Replaced jib with storm jib. Bosham 10.30 hours. Reported to Harbour Master. Returned to find vessel hanging from harbour wall owing to tide fall.

The next two days contained accounts of his peering out to sea and wetting his finger and deciding not to sail. He told me he was having the time of his life and he wished he'd taken up sailing earlier. And I, for one, am not sneering at him.

This inner craving to emulate our adventurous forbears is not, of course, confined to Englishmen. At Einkausen in Holland I met a German who quite obviously dreamed of himself as Wolfgang von Jem Green. He had sailed from Hamburg, and as he told us he was an army officer we promptly nicknamed him General Speidel.

After examining our boat with a contemptuous air he suddenly said, 'Did you sail from England?'

'No,' we replied. 'We hired the boat over here.'

'Perhaps you have fear of the veend?' he suggested. 'My colonel he was coming with me, but he have fear of the veends. And my wife, she have fear. Everyone have fear. I do not have fear. I sail to England tomorrow.'

There was a roll of thunder in the distance. His eyes gleamed.

'Ah, it is good,' he said. 'We have a storm. Tomorrow plenty veend. I go sail to Hastings. You know Hastings, yes?'

He set sail early next morning in a storm of Wagnerian dimensions, with the lightning playing about him, and doubtless humming the 'Ride of the Valkyries'.

The sequel, however, was rather disappointing. Two days later we sailed past him in Amsterdam harbour, where he was obviously moored for some time, since all his underwear was hanging out to dry. He pretended not to see us.

But the year the events described in this book took place I really thought I had escaped sailing. Everything was arranged for a peaceful trip to Budleigh Salterton when Beaver rang up and asked if I would like to come round to his house for a drink that evening.

Beaver is an old sailing friend, a fat, bearded little bachelor of fifty who has nearly cost me my life on many an occasion. He may have a proper name but if so I've never heard it used. I'm quite sure if he were married (an unlikely event) the vicar would have to say, 'Do you, Beaver, take this woman . . .'

When I arrived there was a group of people lying all over the front room examining charts and pretending they understood them. Beaver was having a pre-sailing conference. At these he outlines a preposterous route for the week which would be difficult for a hydroplane to complete, let alone a couple of old sloops. They were all old sailing friends, with one exception: a nervy, not unattractive-looking girl of nineteen, who was introduced to me as Joan. She was the only person who had not sailed before and was bouncing around and asking silly questions like 'Do we have to sit up all night keeping watch or hosing the scuppers?' I told her that the only times when we sat up all night were to drink or when Beaver ran us aground.

'I think it's going to be *fun*,' she squeaked (I was to discover she had a habit of talking like something out of a schoolgirls' annual). Personally, I doubted it, for she was sailing with Dennis and Arthur, two of the most selfish bachelors that ever took a girl sailing so she could peel the spuds. Dennis—a precise, clipped sort of chap, who had been a naval officer in the war and couldn't quite forget it—had already handed Joan a typewritten daily menu which would not have disgraced a first-class hotel. Arthur was talking incessantly in a strange bucolic accent. Nobody knows where he picked it up. He claims it to be a piece of genuine Fen dialect, but it sounds like something left over from the local amateur dramatic society. However, as he is a seed salesman, it sometimes comes in useful with the customers.

Beaver's tame slaves on this trip were to be Harry, who when sailing drinks a bottle of Worthington every morning as soon as he gets up, and his wife Sheila, who spends her time tending their ever-growing brood. After about six gins I became aware that Harry, Sheila and Beaver were treating me as one of the crew, saying things like 'We shall have to have

. . . outlines a preposterous route for the week

steak this year, 'specially for Mike,' the cunning swines. I explained feebly that I was going to Budleigh Salterton, and Beaver said, 'Yes, of course,' and poured me two more gins. By the time he opened a new bottle I actually *wanted* to go on the trip.

Beaver produced a catalogue and showed me the yacht, *Merryweather II*, a worn-out old twenty-eight-foot sloop described as 'ideal for the yachtsman with some practical experience'. This is the middle category on the Broads. The lowest is 'suitable for both novice and experienced yachtsman'.

The catalogue sang the praises of *Merryweather* in lyrical language. 'Roomy saloon,' it warbled (they always call the rabbit-hutch in the middle the saloon), 'with easy-to-raise cabin-top. Third berth in forepeak. Wash-basin. Toilet entirely separate. An extremely comfortable boat. Self-acting jib available.'

Translated into plain words this meant that the cabin-top would lift only under the combined efforts of three strong men, and was liable to collapse on our heads while we were having dinner. It was also liable to slide overboard if we did a violent gybe. The wash-basin was just about big enough to wash one's little finger in. The berth in the forepeak was designed for someone shaped like a letter S. When the cabin roof was lowered the toilet could be used only by a contortionist. The self-acting jib had never in all our experience failed to catch on the burgee halyard cleat as it swung across, and far from saving labour usually required one extra hand whose sole duty was to kick it across every time.

They had also omitted to mention that the bilge pump was broken and seemed to pump water in instead of out, and that every rope on board was in a tangled knot. They might also have added that *Merryweather* sailed with pernicious lee helm. Twenty-odd years ago Beaver used to secure the best and fastest yachts on the Broads, but after a series of disasters he found it increasingly difficult to do so. He tried changing from boatyard to boatyard but his reputation followed him and he finally had to settle for Loudwater's. While it would not be true to say that Mr. Loudwater looked forward to Beaver's annual visits, at least he put up with them, and there was always the consolation that the damage he caused was so extensive that it kept his men occupied during the winter when work was short.

We broke up at midnight and next day I wrote to the guest-house at Budleigh Salterton:

My dear Mrs. Jones,

I am sure you will be sorry to hear that I shall be unable to spend the week of July 15 with you as planned. Yesterday I received news that my guardian has been taken ill in the Shetlands and is expected to pass away some time in the week beginning July 15.

It is indeed a tragic coincidence that this should happen as last summer you may remember I was called to Co. Cork, again to a sick relative's bedside.

Last year you may remember that in view of the unfortunate circumstances you were kind enough to refund my deposit on re-letting the room, and I wonder if you could see your way to do the same this time. Perhaps when you reply you could enclose the camera I left behind in 1959 and about which I have written several times. . . .

Two

ACCORDING to Beaver's military-type schedule I had to report to his home at six-thirty on the first morning of the trip. Much to my surprise I actually arrived by ten to seven. After I had rung the bell for ten minutes his aged aunt appeared and told me her nephew was still sleeping. At that moment a window was flung open upstairs and Beaver stuck out his head and demanded what all the damn' noise was about. I told him and he grunted and shut the window violently. His aunt vanished (she was that sort of woman, she had a knack of becoming invisible at a moment's notice) and I spent my time mooning about the front room looking at photographs of Beaver as a repulsive child.

It was half an hour before Beaver appeared, looking like a walking ships' chandlery, festooned in coils of rope and tottering under the weight of an incredible collection of marine junk ranging from binoculars to a hatchet.

'No breakfast,' he announced firmly. 'I'll get something at Newmarket. We've got to push on.'

Harry and his wife were on their fifth cup of coffee when we arrived. Sheila was looking rather depressed because their children were at her mother-in-law's. Far from depressing Harry, the loss seemed only to uplift him and he made a grateful reference to 'the first bit of peace I've had for five years'.

It took nearly half an hour to load their luggage. That was Sheila's influence. You find that where a man will go sailing cheerfully for a week with just a spare pair of socks, women insist on taking such unnecessary luxuries as an extra corset and, of course, a dress ('in case we should go to a dance'). This gigantic mountain was somehow piled into the luggage rack on top of the car, and with a crash of gears Beaver drove off.

He drove to the end of the street at about fifty miles an hour, braked violently at the corner, and the whole rack shot over the bonnet and nearly hit a policeman on point duty. Harry and I risked death to salvage the stuff, snatching suitcases from under the very wheels of buses. The only casualty was a tube of shaving-cream belonging to Beaver, which was run over by a lorry and squirted all over the policeman's trousers. He didn't notice because his attention was taken up with Beaver, who was snarling and cursing and waving his fists at a queue of hooting cars behind him.

At nine o'clock we started off again. We were very late and Beaver's speed was nightmarish. At least it would have been, but I couldn't see much of what transpired because all the luggage was now inside the car and my view was restricted to one side of a large suitcase nursed on my lap. From Beaver's frequent and succinct comments, however, it was possible to judge that we were making painful progress along a road filled with lunatics and car-driving ordure (a favourite term of Beaver's).

The estimated time of arrival at the boatyard had been ten-thirty. We got there just as the staff went for lunch. *Merryweather II* was clearly not ready to sail. She had not been cleaned and was without blankets and a gas cylinder. Beaver gazed at her in horror and then addressed the boatyard men as they sat munching their sandwiches. In Napoleonic style he begged for volunteers to prepare the yacht as we had a long way to go before nightfall and was rewarded with some encouraging smiles and nods and jerks of the thumb in the direction of the yard office. Nobody moved, however. Harry suggested having a bite to eat but Beaver reacted as if someone had proposed a vote of thanks to the Pope at a Communist Party meeting.

'Sheila—get the stores from the shop,' he barked. 'Mike, help her. Harry, help me check the rigging. We'll sail at fourteen hundred hours.' (Although Beaver used the twenty-four-hour clock to show we were now under command, he would secretly have preferred to say 'four bells'. Unfortunately, he could never remember how many bells meant what.) His little speech, however, was rewarded with a cheer from the boatmen, who had heard it all before.

On the way to the grocery store Sheila drew my attention to a pre-war Ford Eight at the side of the road. 'Should the back of that car be like that?' she asked.

The car in question had an odd gap between the body and the luggage rack. Through this could be seen a female posterior clad in leopard-skin slacks. There was something familiar about those trousers. And sure enough, as we watched, Joan stuck her head out of the window, waved madly, and cried, 'Isn't this *fun*?'

Dennis, whose car it was, tottered from the grocer's carrying a large carton full of wine-bottles.

'Had a bit of bother on the way down,' he explained. 'All that patent metal substitute I fixed round the body gave way suddenly, and old Joan nearly fell out through the back. I'm going to write to the *Autocar* about it. I mean to say, they claim it'll withstand a weight of two tons and Joan doesn't weigh a quarter of that.'

Sheila gave a squeak. 'Oh, look, Dennis, there's a cat in your car.'

'Not you, Joan,' said Dennis, rather unkindly. 'As a matter of fact, it's mine. I couldn't get anyone to take it for the week so I decided to bring it with me.'

I asked him where he was going to keep a cat on a boat and he said airily that he would probably tie him to the mast on a little lead.

'He can swim,' he added. 'I tested him for buoyancy before I went by throwing him in a bath of water and he swam round and round like anything.'

There are times when I'm not sure whether I really like Dennis.

Ten minutes later an extraordinary thing happened. We all found ourselves in the pub. I have noticed this phenomenon before, especially when sailing. I hop ashore for a loaf of bread or something quite innocent and an unseen force drags at my ankles and I find myself marching willy-nilly into the nearest boozer. Harry was already at the bar when we arrived, furtively downing a pint of bitter and peering out of the window to see if Beaver was coming. He had slipped away on the excuse of looking for Loudwater, the boatyard owner, leaving Beaver to grapple with the boat.

What with one thing and another it was closing time when we left. Beaver heard us coming—for some reason we were laughing all over the street—and he was doing a martyr's act making great play of swabbing down the deck with a long-handled mop. He had already set sail (not a particularly safe thing to do in the dyke) and the boom was swinging ominously in the gusts of wind. I noticed that he had exchanged our original quant pole—a long, forked piece of wood used for pushing off and for moving the boat in a calm—for a much larger one, resembling a young flagstaff.

'No time to store that grub,' he shouted. 'Sling it in the cabin and cast off. We're behind schedule already.'

I handed down the packets of food to Harry, who passed them to Sheila inside the cabin. After the first few had been passed Sheila called for Harry to help her and he disappeared below. Beaver ignored the hold-up.

'Cast off for'd,' he boomed impatiently. I shovelled the rest of the stores on to the deck hastily, dropping a jar of pickles into the water. Now I like pickles, so I knelt down to try to fish them out. Beaver paid no attention. 'Cast off aft,' he said firmly, lost in his own dream world. A piece of the bank gave way and my shoulder slipped under as I groped for the pickles under water. Beaver was staring at the top of the mast and nodding wisely to himself.

'We're off,' he shouted. 'Harry, take the jib sheets. Mike, stand by with the quant pole. Sheila, stow the rond anchor. Jump to it everybody.' He sawed the tiller back and forth vigorously. 'She's not making much way. Pull in the port jib sheet, Harry, and, Mike, give her a poke with the quant.'

At this stage I felt obliged to explain something.

'Beaver,' I said, 'we are still tied to the bank.'

Beaver came back to earth from his limbo and looked around in bewildered fashion.

'Tied to the bank? Why are we tied to the bank? We should be in midstream by now.'

Harry appeared in the cabin doorway.

'Sorry I wasn't much help in that little hoo-hah just now,' he explained, 'but Sheila was being sick.'

Beaver growled and made sympathetic noises.

'As a matter of fact,' went on Harry, 'she's not very well. In fact, you see . . . Well, the truth of the matter is that she's going to have a baby.'

There was a momentary silence, broken only by a tiny feminine sound down below. Beaver's eyes widened.

'Going to have a baby? Good God, do you mean *now*?'

'Oh no, not immediately. In about seven months.'

Beaver's relief was perceptible, but he was not mollified.

'You ought to have told me you'd brought a stark raving preggers female on my boat. Preggers, by George. We've never had that happen on the Broads yet, not in all the years I've been coming here.'

'I'm sorry.'

'Well, it can't be helped now,' said Beaver magnanimously. 'You'd better tell her she's excused duty on the jib sheets until she's better.'

'So kind,' said Harry, not without a trace of malice, and went below to comfort Sheila.

An elderly female, one of the boat cleaners, appeared at my ear.

'Excuse me, my dear,' she said, 'but Oi couldn't 'elp overhearing what was said just now. If your friend's wife's 'aving 'er confinement she oughter come ashore, you know. A Broads boat ain't no place for a babby to be born in. Shall Oi phone for the doctor at Ranworth?'

'Do you mind, madam?' interrupted Beaver icily from the cockpit. 'We are about to sail.'

'But that little babby . . .'

'There will be no babby, as you call it, for seven months. But *I* shall have one immediately unless I am allowed to set sail. Nobody seems to realize that we've got to make Yarmouth tonight. Now will someone please cast off fore and aft?'

Having abandoned the pickles as irretrievably lost, I untied the forward line, ran along the bank and cast off the stern as well.

'Right-ho,' shouted Beaver. 'This is it. Grab those jib sheets, Mike. Harry, come up here and stand by with the quant pole. Sheila, don't be sick anywhere except in the lavatory. Jump to it.'

We moved forward three feet and stopped. An aged boatman from the yard had seized our stern rope and taken a turn round a post, and was now looking quizzically at our sails and shaking his head. Beaver nearly exploded with rage.

'Let that rope go, you old fool,' he hooted malevolently.

The old man replied by winding in the rope a little more so that Beaver was subjected to the indignity of travelling backwards with all sail set while he sawed the tiller futilely. Having secured us, the old man said: 'You ain't a-going to sail in this 'ere wind without a double reef, are you? We 'ad one chap back 'ere this morning with a hole in his jib big enough to put your 'ead in.'

'Double reef?' Beaver laughed. 'Double reef? In this breeze? Why, the water's hardly popply.'

The waterman looked sagely up at the trees bending in the wind beyond the boatyard buildings.

'I don't know what Mr. Loudwater'll say if we 'ave to come out tomorrow and put a new stick in 'er.'

The mention of Loudwater, his old enemy, put Beaver really on his mettle.

'That's quite all right, my man. Mr. Loudwater knows me very well.' This was perfectly true, since Beaver had decimated his fleet over the years. 'I may take in a tuck at Thurne Mouth if I think fit. And now would you kindly let go of my stern rope as I have to be at Yarmouth before dark.'

At the mention of Yarmouth the old man shook his head and chuckled. 'Yarmouth, eh? You're a right 'un, you are. Well, don't say I didn't tell you. I don't know what Mr. Loudwater would say if he knew. Off you go, then.' He untied the rope and gave the stern a kick. 'But I'm telling you—you'll never get anywhere like that. Not like that you won't.'

In passing I may say that one always seems to set out on a sailing trip to prognostications of woe from professional watermen. Instead of the cheerful cries of 'Good luck, good sailing', for which one would hope, there is simply a dismal chorus of groans together with uncomplimentary remarks about the set of your sails. I remember once setting out from a yard in Chichester harbour to such a chorus of moans and groans and shaking of heads that I turned back and asked them what was wrong, since I was convinced that at the very least I had pulled the plug out of the bottom of the boat.

They seemed surprised that I was worried and explained they were merely warning me I had a small rope trailing astern. I said it was lucky the coastguard hadn't heard them or the lifeboat would have turned out, but the sarcasm was lost.

But, then, professionals are like that in every walk of life. One would think they didn't *want* trade. There used to be an old boatbuilder in Sussex who had positively to be begged to build a yacht. One of my few wealthy friends once went down there one weekend and airily explained that he wanted a handy little sloop built for next season and he wasn't going to be too choosey about the price.

The old man continued planing a piece of wood.

'You can't just walk in 'ere and ask me to build you a boat like that,' he said. 'Oh dearie me, no. I've got to find out whether I'm going to like you first. I wouldn't have one of my boats sailed by someone I didn't like the look of.'

'Well, what the hell do you want me to *do*?' asked my friend, flabbergasted.

'Just you come on down here every so often and ask me again,' replied the old man, still planing. 'Then we'll see if I can build you a boat.'

Well, my friend kept on going down there nearly every weekend for six months, and then just as his patience was exhausted the old man said quietly one day: 'No, I shan't build you a boat. I'm too busy.' My friend says that it was only by a superhuman effort he refrained from pouring a pot of glue over the old chap's head.

My garage is like that. I drove my old car in there once with a mudguard hanging off and asked them to weld it. One would have thought I'd blasphemed or something. They all looked at me as if I were mad.

'I shall 'ave to get the welder down from Hanwell,' said the proprietor at length, talking as if Hanwell was in the Antipodes instead of six bus-stops up the road.

'Then get him,' I said. 'I can't drive with the mudguard hanging.'

He pondered this.

'You're sure you wouldn't prefer to take it to Smith's?' he insisted.

'No,' I said. 'Smith's are thieves.'

'All right,' he announced reluctantly. 'But the welder's not going to come for nothing, you know. It's five pound as soon as he puts his goggles on.'

I can never get away with that sort of blackmail. When a newspaper requires some article from me I only wish the editor would say to his assistant: 'We shall have to get Green from Hanwell. And he's not going to come for nothing. It's five pound as soon as he unscrews his fountain-pen.'

Instead of which, I have a shrewd belief that they really say: 'Oh, get old Mike Green to do it. He'll write anything for a beer and a couple of guineas.'*

'Old goat,' muttered Beaver, as we ghosted quietly down the dyke. 'Telling me when to put in a reef!' At that moment we passed from the shelter of the boatyard sheds and screamed round into the main river to a crash of breaking crockery and a cry of 'What the hell?' from Harry, who stuck a worried head out of the cabin.

We were off.

Despite everything, the departure was comparatively peaceful for Beaver. The previous year he had been so impatient that he had loaded someone else's stores on the boat and set sail with them. This was discovered after two hours, but Beaver refused to return, partly because the stranger's stores were much better than his own and included some particularly nice wine. However, the indignant rightful owner pursued him in one of Loudwater's launches and forced him to give up the luxuries in exchange for his own miserable provisions.

It became clear within an hour that we were not going to make Yarmouth. The wind was dead ahead and so violent and flukey that time after time we failed to come round at the end of a tack and were blown ignominiously into the trees by the river, whence Harry and I extricated us with the quant pole. There was nothing new in the situation for any of us. It is just one of the hazards of Broads ditch-crawling. But I couldn't help wishing Beaver had double-reefed.

* If anyone *really* believes that, they want their head examining.

Sheila recovered after a time and came up to make some tea. Beaver peered at her sideways in an odd fashion. He had a fear of women, whom he regarded as unnatural creatures, and

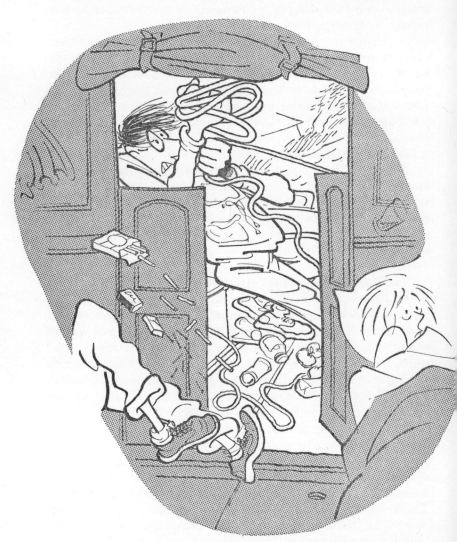

. . . passed from the shelter of the boatyard sheds

to have a woman on board who was expecting a baby caused him the greatest distress. I think he regarded her as a female Jonah.

Cooking on *Merryweather II* was not easy. Like many Broads boats, she had the stove in a locker under a seat in the well, and access was gained by lifting the seat. Just as the kettle was boiling we blew into a tree and during the ensuing confusion Beaver plunged his leg into the cooking locker and leapt four feet into the air as a jet of steam went up his trouser leg. After that tea was banned and we opened a few cans of beer instead.

That sort of thing is inseparable from cooking under way, especially if the food is stored in thwart lockers. The usual thing that happens is that Cook opens one of the leeside lockers while the vessel is on one tack, tries to grab everything before the boat comes about, and fails, so that as you heel over the other way a cascade of jam-jars, bean tins and detergent packets streams across the deck. I recall going aground for five hours because the helmsman put his bare foot in a pound of butter and fell flat on his back.

Not only that, but we couldn't use the butter. We did make a tentative try but one look at the helmsman's foot decided us against it.

It was almost dark when we reached Thurne Mouth, where the River Thurne joins the Bure. Normally Yarmouth would be at least five hours' sailing away. Harry pointed this out to Beaver, who showed no sign of having heard and merely asked him to haul the jib sheet tighter. But just as we rounded the corner Sheila exclaimed, 'Look at that funny man over there!'

Through the gloom a dim figure could be discerned jumping up and down and waving his arms. And then it spoke, and the ghastly bucolic accent was unmistakable. It was Arthur.

'Boyur,' he boomed (Arthur always begins with a vague mooing sound when excited), 'why don't yew throw me a loin?'

'What's that about his loins?' asked Beaver. 'Is he in trouble of some sort?' We explained that Arthur wanted us to throw him a mooring-rope. Beaver looked even more puzzled.

'Mooring-rope?' he repeated. 'Why isn't he trying to make Yarmouth? He's not aground, is he?'

Arthur joined in from the bank, his voice indistinct in the rising gale.

'Boyur . . . yew'll never make Yarmouth tonight . . . too dark . . . gale blowing up . . . death . . . destruction all round. . . .'

Beaver pondered this for a moment and said suddenly, 'Tell him we'll make for Potter Heigham instead.'

Harry bellowed the reply as we turned violently. We never heard Arthur's comments because Beaver swung the boat round in a dizzy gybe and we found ourselves setting off up the River Thurne in what was now nearly a howling gale, but I saw *Quiet Dawn* being cast off as we sped round the bend.

It was almost pitch dark when we reached Potter, although fortunately the wind had slackened with the coming of darkness. Coming alongside and mooring should have been the work of a few moments. But not for dear old Beaver, who insisted that a simple rearrangement of all the boats moored by the bank would mean a clear space for us.

Within five minutes the river was a seething mass of craft. Those with no one aboard were unceremoniously cast loose and towed to new positions while Beaver in person visited all the other boats, explaining why he wanted them to move. He received one or two rude answers. By the time it was all over there was a gigantic trot of six boats moored abreast while *Merryweather II* reclined in solitary state by the bank. Two motor-cruisers had their lines tangled and were drifting about the river helplessly. To make matters worse, people were returning from the pub and finding their boats had gone and creating a terrific caterwauling, shining torches and crying out in anger.

One or two people, not knowing their craft had been moved, boarded the wrong boats. I sympathized with their predicament, for I once got on the wrong yacht in Oulton Broad. It was a sister-yacht to my own and I had actually crawled into the forepeak to fetch something before I discovered my mistake. I was just about to leave when the boat rocked as two people came aboard and then I heard a man's voice say, 'It's all right, darling, there's no one here.'

I remained frozen with embarrassment.

A woman then said, 'Are you sure it's safe, Adrian?'

'Of course,' came the reply, a little too heartily, I felt. 'No one will find us here.'

'Oh, Adrian, I can't help thinking this is wrong. It seems so mean. What about Charles?'

'What about him? From what you've told me he . . .'

At this point I could stand it no longer and coughed loudly. There was a pregnant silence and then the woman began to scream: 'I knew it, I knew it. Charles is on board. He's waiting for us. He's got his old Service revolver with him. Oh, Adrian, why did we do it? Why, why, why?'

This geezer Adrian didn't exactly seem to be the heroic type because at the mention of the word 'revolver' he left the boat in two strides. The woman was not far behind. When I was certain they were out of sight I crept forth and scurried back to my own yacht.

Fortunately nothing like that happened this time, but just when the confusion was at its height *Quiet Dawn* arrived with a shout of 'Boyur' from Arthur and came alongside the line of six boats which now resembled a small pontoon bridge across the river.

Beaver surveyed the chaos with satisfaction.

'It's much better when you organize things,' he said. 'Let's go and have a drink.'

Three

THE last thing I remember hearing before going to sleep was an ominous howling of the wind in the rigging and Beaver saying, 'Don't forget, six o'clock start tomorrow for Yarmouth.'

I was awakened by an insistent tapping on the shelf at the bottom of the bunk. It sounded as if someone were dropping a small pebble every few seconds. I heaved myself half upright and my thighs touched part of the bedding that was wet and cold. At the same time I became aware that it was raining cats and dogs outside and the wind was shrieking devilishly. It was pitch dark and the luminous alarm, set for the early start, showed three-twenty.

The cabin light revealed pools of water on the shelf, where a drip from the roof was tapping monotonously. There was a small pool of water on the side of my blankets. I was pleased to see there was also a pool on Beaver's blankets and a drip descending on the end of his beard as he lay on his back. I rather hoped a drip might go into his open mouth.

Up on the deck something seemed to have carried away. There was a slap-slapping of metal against the cabin roof. What with the gloom, the wind's howling, the splashing, and a soft snoring from Harry on the floor, the cabin was a dismal and eerie place.

I swung my legs over the side of the bunk and trod on Harry's face. He emitted a stifled snort and bit my big toe. Beaver awoke, stared wildly about him and sat up crying, 'Cast her off . . . cast her off.' We never found out what he meant.

'It's all right,' I said soothingly. 'I think we've got a shackle swinging loose. I'm just going up on deck.'

'I'm all wet,' said Beaver plaintively.

'So am I,' said Harry, who was only semi-conscious. 'Who's been throwing water all over the cabin?'

'Damn stupid trick, that, throwing water all over the place,' mumbled Beaver, falling asleep at the end of the sentence and then waking up again. 'Ought to have more sense.'

I went on deck to be met by a blast of wind and rain which nearly knocked me overboard. I saw that the noise was being caused by the shackle on the end of the jib halyard which I had loosely tied round a shroud and which had worked loose in the gale. Knots are not my strong point. Ever since we found ourselves drifting through Yarmouth harbour at two o'clock in the morning Beaver has refused to let me make the boat fast and I must say I don't blame him.

Just as I retied the halyard, Beaver came up on deck. 'The cabin's leaking like a sieve,' he moaned. 'I bet old Loudwater's done it deliberately because he knew I'd be having the boat. I've half a mind to stop the cheque I paid him.'

We carefully examined the cabin-top. The water seemed to be possessed of some supernatural power by which it could force itself through a solid cabin roof. Not only that, but it kept leaking in different places, now sending down a small waterfall near the wall and then squirting a stream of rain in the centre. The whole contraption gave a pretty fair imitation of a tea-strainer.

While we were looking round, the sound of voices came from the forepeak beneath our feet where Sheila was sleeping. Beaver was standing on the forepeak hatch and I was just about to suggest raising the hatch when it was opened from below by Harry.

I say opened, but he lifted it only about six inches at one side. It was enough. Beaver tottered backwards, waving his arms and jerking his legs up and down as in a ghastly, nightmarish march, and vanished over the side.

He hit the water just as Harry put his head out of the hatch and said: 'Who's the idiot who's standing on the hatch? I couldn't get it open.'

Surprisingly, Beaver took the whole affair quite calmly. He

was almost embarrassing in his determination to forgive and forget. Sheila, foolish girl, insisted upon giving up her bed for him, which was rather illogical because now the wettest person on the boat had the driest bed, while the driest (i.e. Sheila) had to have a wet bed. However, we arranged ourselves with Beaver in the forepeak, Harry on the floor and Sheila in Beaver's bunk. We had all settled down to troubled slumber when the boat rocked violently as someone came on deck, and Arthur opened the cabin door.

'Boyur,' he bawled, nearly cracking our eardrums. 'I just thought I'd warn yew that it's raining and blowing outside, so yew want to watch for leaks in that there cabin roof.'

We thanked him politely and said we hadn't noticed the rain but now he mentioned it there did seem to be a slight inclemency of the weather. Sarcasm is wasted on Arthur, however. Harry suggested Arthur might like to tell Beaver in the forepeak, in case he hadn't heard, and he clumped off happily to do so. I heard him lift the hatch and then there came the sound of it being suddenly closed and a shout as if someone had caught his fingers.

We saw no more of Arthur that night.

Dawn came after what seemed a damp eternity. Soon after six Beaver's alarm went off but Harry silenced it by throwing it out of the cabin and a rumbling from the forepeak showed that its owner slept on undisturbed. That was more than we were doing, racked as we were by cramps through trying to curl up on the dry parts of the bedclothes. Sheila had got so wet she had climbed into bed with Harry on the floor. I must say it made me feel uncomfortable. It gave me rather a shock to turn and find her face about six inches from mine. For one ghastly moment I thought she had got into the wrong bunk and I should appear in the newspapers under a heading like

£5,000 DAMAGES AGAINST 'YACHT MONSTER'

'A Likely Tale'—Judge.

It rather reminded me of an incident in the Army when I visited a friend in another unit and was offered an unoccupied bunk for the night in a barrack room. At 3 a.m. two military policemen marched in and asked where Davis slept. A sleepy hand was waved at my bunk and before I knew what was happening I was being frog-marched across to the guardroom clad only in a shirt.

Naturally, I didn't go in silence. 'You can't do this to me,' I squawked. 'I don't belong here, I'm a Hussar. I know your colonel's batman very well. I'll get you into trouble, you'll see.'

They merely continued to drag me along, muttering: 'All right, Davis, you've led us a merry dance but we aren't going to let you escape again. This time you'll get three years.'

I demanded to see the guard commander, but he was asleep (an offence for which he could have been shot, I may say) and I was bundled into a cell where I spent the rest of the night hammering on the door like someone in an American penitentiary.

It was all sorted out at Reveille. I often wonder whether they caught the real Davis and what he had done.

Sheila brought me back to the present by complaining that she wanted to be sick.

Now this raised an awkward point. The lavatory was in the forepeak where Beaver lay asleep. Not to put too fine a point on it, the apparatus was a mere eighteen inches from his head. Before we could ask him to move, poor Sheila made an urgent effort to open the cabin doors, which promptly jammed, and then dived into the forepeak.

I don't think I have ever heard such language used to a woman before. Even Harry, who could not be accused of being the most attentive of husbands, was moved to protest, 'I say, Beaver, old boy, turn it up a bit.'

Eventually Beaver burst from the forepeak hatch, honking like a flock of wild geese and crying: 'My God, isn't it enough getting pushed overboard in the middle of the night without having some woman vomiting by my bunk in the morning. It's never happened to me all the years I've been sailing . . . never, never. Is this a boat or a maternity ward, that's what I want to know?'

There was nothing to do but ignore him, so we started to prepare breakfast. We were all on our hands and knees in the well, groping in puddles of water in the food lockers, when

Arthur and Dennis arrived and demanded audience with Beaver, who was marching along the bank, sniffing the air and muttering, 'Preggers, by God!'

'Boyur,' said Arthur, by way of greeting. 'We presume yew aren't thinking o' setting sail today, at least not till this 'ere wind's gone down a bit?'

Beaver reared aggressively. 'Nonsense,' he said firmly. 'It's nothing. Just a little morning blow, that's all.' A gust blew off Arthur's hat as he spoke. 'We're going to start as soon as we've finished breakfast. We'll never make Yarmouth at this rate. We're six hours behind schedule already.'

'Actually,' put in Dennis, in his precise way, 'it's at least Force Nine on the Beaufort Scale.' He produced a tattered yachting handbook. 'According to *Worthing's Yachting for Everyman*, this is defined as "Slight structural damage occurs (chimney-pots and slates blown off)".'

'Well, I can't see any chimney-pots being knocked off,' retorted Beaver. 'Does your book say anything about "Broads boats lay up wasting time at Potter Heigham all day"?'

'No, but it says something about skippers who set sail at their peril.'

'Nonsense. You'd better hurry up if you don't want to be left behind.'

'We'll let you know after breakfast.'

Our own breakfast was a miserable affair. Sheila couldn't face frying food in her delicate condition, and Harry did most of the cooking. Harry is not the best of cooks. In fact, it would be no exaggeration to say that he is probably the worst cook in Europe. His idea of frying an egg is to beat it with savage force against some hard object such as the deck and then to scrape up the remains with a knife and let them drip into the pan. He likes his bacon almost raw. I like mine well done. I got it almost raw. However, to compensate presumably, there was about half a pound of black fried filth mixed up with my egg, so I suppose I shouldn't complain.

Midway through the proceedings the Calor gas blew out unnoticed and filled the boat with a nauseous stench. Beaver was terrified. He insisted that the gas, being heavier than air, would sink into the bilge and explode later in the voyage. He recalled a night at Burnham-on-Crouch when a boat blew up and drifted blazing on to the other craft, like one of Drake's fireships which dismayed the Armada off Calais.

The upshot of all this was that we had to get up the deck-boards and *bale* the gas out. I have rarely seen anything more absurd than two grown men solemnly baling nothing out of the bottom of a yacht and carefully tipping it over the side.

Two small boys on a motor-cruiser came and watched us and called out, 'Mummy, look at those funny men on that boat.' Beaver growled at them a good old nautical term for 'go away' and they repeated this to their mother in all innocence.

A man's voice—presumably that of their father—joined the conversation from the cruiser's cabin, saying loudly, 'Tell that man if he says that to you again I'll come over with a boat-hook.'

I rather admired Beaver's retort. 'It's all right,' he said, 'we've got a boathook, thanks.'

Fortunately, the outraged parent did not appear to hear.

After our apology for breakfast I walked to the famous old bridge for a packet of cigarettes and passed Arthur's boat. It was an irritating sight. Inside the cabin Arthur and Dennis were sprawled in slippered ease, stroking the cat, while Joan, dirty, wet and with her hair all over her face, knelt over the stove like a slavey.

'Joan,' called Dennis from the cabin. 'There's no cherry on my grapefruit.' She left the egg she was cooking and hunted round in the well for a cherry. When she returned to the frying-pan the egg was looking rather leathery.

'Boyur,' called out Arthur. 'Yew know how I loikes my eggs, don't yew, me dear? I likes 'em crisp round the outside and underdone in the middle.'

Joan looked helplessly at the mess in front of her and then tipped the egg over the side and started afresh.

'Hurry up, me dear,' called Arthur, 'I've finished my grapefruit.'

Joan looked up bravely, determined to enjoy it all.

'I say, Mike,' she said, 'isn't this fun?'

Beaver and Harry were already untying the sails when I

returned to *Merryweather II*. The wind howled dismally over the flat fields, and moaned in the telephone wires. Hardly anyone was about. A man in a yacht moored astern peered sleepily from under his awning and watched in a startled fashion as we prepared to set sail.

When all was ready Beaver marched down to *Quiet Dawn* and delivered an ultimatum.

'Are you sailing?' he demanded.

'I think we'll stay here and see how yew get on,' said Arthur, his mouth full of fried egg. 'If yew seem to be doing all right, then we'll follow on. Then if yew gets into trouble getting under way we can help yew, can't we?'

Dennis added: 'Have a cup of coffee. And by the way, Joan, there were some bits in the last lot. Can't stand coffee with bits in it.'

Joan rolled her eyes wildly.

Beaver refused coffee and we went back to *Merryweather*, now swinging violently in the wind, which was gusting viciously. Harry looked troubled.

'It's blowing up, you know, Beaver,' he said. 'Don't you think we ought to wait?'

As he spoke a gull blew past, going backwards.

Beaver ignored the query. 'Just stand by to cast off, Mike,' he replied. 'Harry, get on the jib sheets. Sheila, keep out of the way.'

It is never particularly easy getting away from Potter Heigham. The river is only about sixty feet wide and there are boats moored each side. On this occasion the wind was dead ahead, and until we cast off we didn't realize how strong it was. A violent gust caught *Merryweather II*, the boat heeled over until the side-decking was under water and every food locker on the windward side fell open, so a cascade of eggs rolled across the well. Beaver trod on one and sat down suddenly. *Merryweather* shot across the narrow channel like a dart and smote a motor-cruiser moored on the opposite bank.

I have experienced many collisions on the Broads. They're inevitable on those crowded waterways. But I have never experienced one in which there was so much noise.

The shock of the collision knocked me flat on the cabin roof,

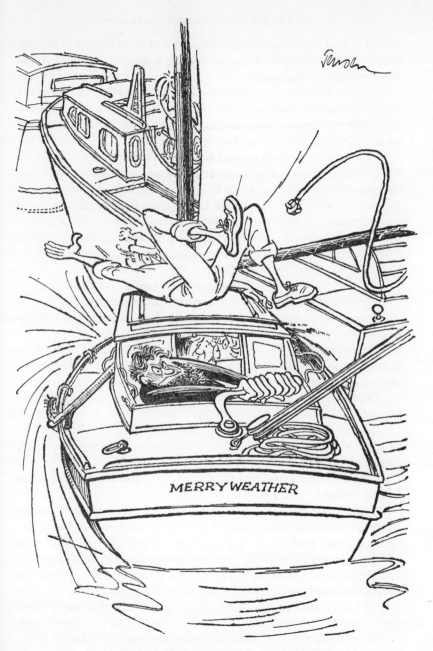

. . . shot across the narrow channel like a dart

where I had been standing, clinging to the mast. As I got up my ears were assailed by a deafening female squawking from the bowels of the cruiser.

Then a terribly Kensington accent said loudly, 'Are you all right, Mothah?' This was followed by more squawking and a clean-limbed young specimen of English manhood climbed up on deck, tying a silk scarf round his neck.

We sheered off and started to blow sideways down the river towards the bridge. I got one arm round the forestay and one leg on another boat to try to bring the head round, and found myself in imminent danger of being split in half. Beaver was bawling a series of utterly incomprehensible and useless orders such as 'Back the jib . . . quant on the port side . . . tell that boat to get out of the way. . . .' The boat in question, incidentally, had been moored for four days.

Young Kensington watched us in a bewildered fashion.

'Why don't you start your engine?' he called out.

Beaver appeared about to burst, but merely said some people preferred not to have them.

Harry saved the day by throwing the forward line to a kindly cruiser skipper. I got the jib down without waiting for orders and we tied to the cruiser for a respite.

Beaver then asked, 'Why is that woman roaring with laughter?'

'She is not,' Harry told him. 'She is screaming hysterically in that cruiser in front. I don't think she appreciated being rammed by you.'

Clean Limbs appeared on deck again and piped, 'Mothah is very upset.'

'I don't wonder,' shouted Beaver. 'Mooring in that stupid place. It was obvious someone would want to tack across there.'

A further terrible outburst came from below. Mother was calling violently for Rodney, who was apparently her offspring. He disappeared, looking very worried. Sheila, who throughout everything had been crawling on the floor of the well trying to salvage food and was now scraping up detergent from a burst packet, started to take an interest.

'I really do think you ought to go and see if that poor woman's all right,' she said. 'She sounds frightful.'

36

'Of course the old cow's all right!' (Beaver talking.) 'What's she worrying about, anyway?' A thought occurred to him suddenly. 'She's not pregnant too, is she?'

Sheila ignored the crude remark. 'Well, I'm going to see how she is. And I think you ought to come too.'

'No, I won't.'

'Yes, you will. Harry, Mike, he ought to go, oughtn't he?'

'Yes.'

'Yes.'

'No.'

'Well, will you go if we all go?'

'All right, but you're wasting your time. We ought to be at Yarmouth by now.'

Mother turned out to be stout and middle-aged. She was reclining on a bunk with young Kensington tending her when we got aboard. As soon as our party entered the cabin she set up a piercing scream at the sight of Beaver and could be quieted only when he had left the cabin, after which he remained lurking outside, breathing heavily and muttering to himself.

Beaver had come aboard carrying a sheaf of accident reports which he requested the son to fill in. There was a slight hiatus when it came to the section *Whom do you consider responsible for the accident?*

Young Kensington simply wrote down the name of our boat so Beaver replied by firmly writing: *Act of God.* Later he was to receive a letter from the boatyard addressed to Mr. God.

Mother would not be pacified. 'I knew we should never have come,' she wailed at Rodney. 'I told you we should have gone to Cromer.'

Beaver became tired of staying outside and pushed his great, ugly, bearded mug round the door.

'Madam,' he boomed. 'Where is your husband?'

This produced a most interesting effect. The woman voided herself of an immense screech and young Kensington burst into tears.

'My father,' said Rodney, between sobs, 'has gone off with Another Woman. I have taken Mothah on this cruise to recuperate.'

There seemed nothing more we could do. We silently slunk from the cabin, Beaver muttering, with what he no doubt meant as rough tenderness: 'I'm sorry about your husband, madam. I hope he comes back soon. But just remember there's plenty of pebbles on the beach.'

As soon as we were back on board *Merryweather*, Beaver was faced with mutiny. Harry stepped forward, clutching his forelock, and said, with a mock naval air, 'Beggin' yer pardon, yer honour, but the crew 'ave decided not to sail till the weather moderates.'

'Ha, ha,' replied Beaver. 'Jolly funny. Now if you'll just get the jib up we can head her round and . . .'

We explained gently but firmly that we were not going to sail, and quanted *Merryweather* back across the river. Even that was an achievement in that wind. Beaver immediately sat down with his tide tables to see if we could sail after lunch.

The crew of *Quiet Dawn* were sitting in the well, sipping cocktails and munching pickled cucumbers.

'Boyur,' called out Arthur. 'We saw your old spot of bother. I told Beaver he wouldn't sail out here today and I was right.'

'Joan,' said Dennis, 'there's no cherry in this cocktail. And put some more gin in it while you're about things.'

Joan stuck her head out of the cabin door, her hands covered in potato peelings, and took Dennis's glass, giving me a look which had a touch of wildness about it.

'I say, Mike!' she exclaimed. 'I watched you hit that cruiser. Isn't it all fun?'

The River Thurne flowed quietly on.

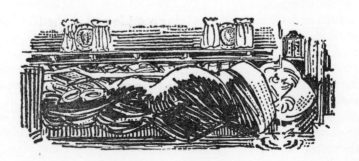

SOME USEFUL KNOTS

The Time Knot: Discovered by accident when I tied up the boat on a short line, and remembered three hours later that the tide fell six feet. On returning I found with relief that the knot had given sufficiently to allow the rope to pay out the right amount. The knot is tied as follows: Form a bight in the rope and slip it over the mooring-post. Then take the fall and make a loop round the standing part. Hold this loop in position with one

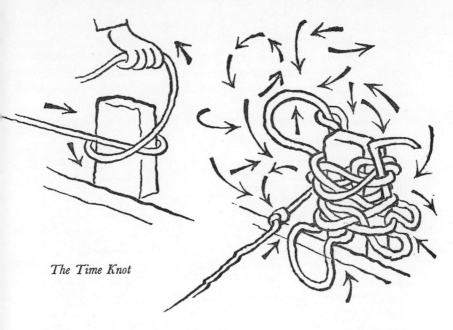

The Time Knot

hand and with the other hand pull the boat in a little to gather some slack and make another loop further down. Keeping the two loops in position, lift the original bight from the post with your teeth (or a third hand if you are so blessed) and pass it through the first loop. Carefully holding everything in position, walk slowly round the post four times. Place one foot against the rope to hold it in position (remembering all the time not to let go of your three loops) and walk round in the other direction. Then one by one drop the loops over the post.

The Granny Clove: A splendid knot for tying up someone else's boat (preferably someone you hate). Can also be used for holding up trousers. Pick up the fall of the mooring-rope and wind it twice round the post (be careful not to wind it round your

The Granny Clove

leg as well or the skipper may be faced with a choice between you and the boat). Flick the end of the fall over the standing part, whirl it round a bit, stand up casually wiping your hands and say firmly, 'O.K., Skipper, she's fast now.' It is best to stand on the rope until everyone is out of sight.

The Mungle

The Mungle: For tying up mutinous members of the crew. An old tea-clipper knot. Wind the rope once round the waist of the offending seaman, pass one end to a colleague and both pull from opposite directions until the mutiny ceases.

Four

AT TWELVE O'CLOCK we all went up to the pub, except Joan, who had to stay behind and watch over some exotic dish that Dennis had ordered for lunch, and Sheila, who as a fellow-member of the Consolidated Women's Trade Union kindly offered to stay and help her. Beaver arrived at the pub carrying an armful of charts and tide tables which he spread all over the bar.

'Now then,' he said, 'we shall have the tide against us after Acle Bridge so we can't waste any time. We've got to start as soon as possible—preferably after this beer.'

'Beaver,' said Dennis, 'look at those trees outside.' They were bending low as the wind whistled through them and at that moment a local opened the door and a violent gust blew all Beaver's charts on to the floor.

'Boyur,' said Arthur. 'Yew can't sail in this. Look what happened this morning.'

'It was all the fault of that stupid old cow in the cruiser. Fancy mooring there! It was obvious we should have to tack out.'

'Perhaps,' said Harry quietly, 'they moored there so as to be near the bank.'

This subtlety was lost on Beaver but we made the point. He agreed to wait until the wind moderated, provided he did not have to spend another night at Potter Heigham. When we were on our third pint the girls arrived, looking tousled and windswept. Joan was showing signs of mutiny. Asked what she wanted to drink, she replied hysterically, 'A double gin,' and gave vent to a maniacal laugh.

'I hope,' said Dennis firmly, 'that you remembered to fry

the meat until it was brown before putting it in the saucepan? And did you hang the bottle of wine over the side to cool?'

Joan's reply was to drain her gin-and-tonic in one gulp and giggle foolishly. I have seen the signs before in girls who go sailing. They start the holiday full of fun and pep, lured by advertisements which promise them a week of sunbathing on the cabin roof while the yacht heels to the exhilarating breeze. After the first day, when they are wet through, tired of cooking on their knees, raw with pulling on ropes, and probably feeling slightly sick, they change their minds. Whenever a girl asks me what she should wear to go cruising I always tell her to put on something which is proof against hot fat.

We stayed in the bar too long and were all foolishly bold with drink when we came out. When Beaver said, 'Right, then it's agreed we have a quick lunch and sail immediately,' not a voice was raised in dissent, although we were standing by a newspaper placard which said:

60 M.P.H. GALE HAVOC IN NORFOLK.

The famous old bridge at Potter, near which we were moored, is very low and narrow. Yachts have to lower their masts to pass under, and even motor-cruisers have to drop superstructure such as hoods and windscreens. While we were eating lunch a cruiser driven by a woman tried to pass through the bridge at full speed, hit the arch and sent the entire cabin roof flying back over the stern.

How we all laughed! I have never seen Beaver so amused. I thought he would choke. There's nothing like seeing someone else in trouble when you're sailing to buck you up. We just sat back and howled.

Our mirth was cut short when an aged human body was seen to be bobbing up and down in the water at the cruiser's stern, hopelessly tangled up in a rope. He had apparently been sitting on the stern and had been swept off.

To say I am no hero would be an understatement. When duty calls and danger you will find old Green hovering in the background suggesting a compromise. But even I got as far as taking off my shoes before diving in when we were stopped by a shout from a local waterman who nipped into an outboard dinghy and pursued the cruiser, still heading full tilt upstream with the old man bobbing like a porpoise behind it.

We rushed to the bridge in time to see the old boy being hauled out and disentangled by the waterman. He gave unmistakable signs of life by launching into a violent tirade against his daughter-in-law, who had been driving the boat (driving being the only appropriate word). Now that there was a happy ending we enjoyed a further good laugh.

Our lunch was a frugal meal of pork pies, but over in *Quiet Dawn* they had a big spread and asked us to sail first so that they could finish the wine. This time Beaver declined to risk sailing across the river and we quanted past the moored boats. The wind was really too strong even for that. As soon as one pulled the quant from the water at the stern the boat's head fell away and she blew sideways towards the bridge.

Normally I quite like quanting, despite the constant drip of water down your sleeve and the danger of falling in. There's a solid satisfaction about it as you walk along the deck with the pole pressed into your shoulder. Indeed, at times I have been known to refer to the quant pole as 'my bride' and to speak ecstatically of my beloved. But today I got a large splinter in my hand ('Your darling bit you,' as Harry put it) and a crowd of ghoulish spectators gathered in their raincoats on the bridge scenting trouble and making fatuous remarks like 'Dad, why is that boat going sideways?' There was not another boat, powered or sail, under way. Everyone was battened down under awnings, listening to the wind's screaming and the occasional pattering of fine rain on the canvas.

Arthur and Dennis had finished their wine when we crawled past and were on to liqueurs and cheroots. All I saw of Joan was her backside sticking out of the cabin as she searched for Dennis's tobacco pouch, so I gave her a cheery hail and was rewarded by an unintelligible noise which sounded as if one of the words were 'fun'.

Arthur gave us an ominously sly grin and called out, 'Boyur, we'll let yew get well clear before we start moving.'

Beaver planned to set sail at the end of the moored boats, where bungalows and trees provide some shelter from the wind

Normally I quite like quanting . . .

and there is more room to manœuvre. We had just started to
hoist when a sullen-looking employee of a local boatyard, who
had been watching from the other bank, shouted, 'You ain't
going to sail in this, are yer?'

'Yes,' said Beaver.

'I forbid you to sail,' came the reply. 'You must be blamed mad. You come down 'ere of a holiday time, mucking about the river as if you was driving a crane. . . .'

This stung Beaver.

'I commanded three hundred men like you in the war,' he interrupted. That was slightly slanderous, because although Beaver *had* commanded three hundred men they had been savage levies mounted on mules. But the man was equal to the remark.

'Ah,' he said, 'and I shot three hundred men like you in the war. And any of 'em could have handled a boat better'n you.'

The argument was cut short as Harry cast us off and dived inboard as *Merryweather II* swung round under the jib.

That first hair-raising charge across the river was a little emoting, as they say, but this time we had room to come about and make another tack. Beaver was at the helm, Sheila was on the jib sheets, Harry was lighting cigarettes for us all and I was in the bows coiling ropes and keeping an eye out for obstructions.

The first of these was a large, six-berth yacht, manned by four young lads, shooting upriver under bare poles and out of control. At first we thought it must have an engine, but as we passed one of the boys called out, 'How can we stop this thing?' They went out of sight round a bend and in the distance there was a cry of 'Boyur' and the sight of a mast waving madly. Most gratifying.

The next vessel was another yacht, also out of control, but this one *had* an engine. There were a man and a woman on board and they'd left the cabin awning up. The gusts of wind were too strong for the puny outboard engine with all that freeboard and they were breezing sideways along the centre of the river, wringing their hands (having an auxiliary engine does that to people, they just sit helpless when the wretched thing won't work). I had no doubt that we should see them later in the trip with the engine working at full speed and all sails set. We just scraped round their bows and advised them to set the jib, or, as Harry explained, 'That little triangular sail at the front.'

About a quarter of a mile downstream there was an eerie drop in the wind. The moaning in the trees died away and there was an utter silence. Beaver cut short his tack to avoid a gentleman driving a motorized dinghy down the centre of the river and *Merryweather* shivered uncomfortably as we came into wind. Next moment a huge gust tore across the water, whipping a little spiral from the surface, and as we paid off it hurled us towards a bungalow running down to the waterside. Beaver put the helm down but it was too late. *Merryweather* would not respond in time.

From my perch in the bows I had an excellent view of a perfect family picture as we headed for the bungalow's french windows. It was the sort of vision politicians paint of the average happy British home. It would have brought tears to the eyes of anyone who had seen it. There was Father, a baldish forty, smoking a pipe and reading the *News of the World*. Grandfather dozed in a corner. The wife was knitting, while a whitehaired old granny was reading the other half of the *News of the World* (the bit with the dirty court cases) and tut-tutting to herself as she gloated over the more sordid aspects. A delightful golden-haired girl of eight played on the carpet with a gurgling baby. The fire blazed cheerfully.

The scene changed in an instant as Mother looked up and saw a four-ton sloop, with a long, pointed bowsprit, hurtling towards the french windows. I heard nothing, but in mime saw the whole lot of them fixed in horror as *Merryweather* bore down.

I thought the bowsprit would go through the television set. Actually it didn't quite reach the windows, as it rode over the wooden piling at the end of the lawn and we were stopped violently by the bobstay digging deep into the rotten wood.

Inside the bungalow, if pandemonium did not reign, it certainly had a working majority. There was an impression of waving arms and legs and then five pairs of eyes were staring through the windows (the baby wasn't watching). On the boat all was order and calm. Everyone was lying flat on their faces and the yacht was fixed firmly by the bow.

I hopped ashore and made ingratiating noises at the family. Father was trying to open the doors without much success, so I hoped to be able to hurry away before we became involved in any more trouble. I pushed against the bow but nothing happened. Finally I lay on my back and pushed the bow with my feet. Still nothing happened. The bobstay remained firmly wedged in the piling.

The doors opened at last and Father stepped forth, followed by his brood. The little golden-haired girl, I noticed, looked much less attractive now. She had an evil expression and was chanting, 'Wasn't it naughty, Mummy, wasn't it naughty of that man to do that?' The old grandfather was chuntering something about 'them blamed schooners careering about the canal'. But Father was of a more forgiving disposition. He knew all about the river. Didn't he come down from Leicester every year to the waterside bungalow?

'Stop grizzling, Phoebe,' he commanded the infant. 'Can I give you a shove?' I asked him to put his hand firmly on the bow and push with all his might while I did the same. We pushed. Nothing happened. Father took off his coat, got his shoulder against the boat, leaned at a fearful angle and pushed even more heartily. This time he fell flat on his face.

'It's no good, Beaver,' I called. 'We're stuck. We're aground on this bungalow.'

'Nonsense.'

Beaver came ashore with Harry. We all pushed, and even Grandfather joined in, but all that happened was that Grandfather dropped his spectacles and for one agonizing moment they hung poised on the edge of the river before Harry rescued them. Following that crisis the family retired, except for Father, who hung about making futile suggestions such as 'Why don't you unscrew that long stick poking out of the front?' (He meant the bowsprit, I think. Or perhaps he meant Harry.)

As far as I can see we should still be there if an angel of mercy had not arrived in the shape of a river inspector. Even he was puzzled at first—he had never known the like—but then he had a brainwave, took out a saw and removed a piece of the piling. This meant we had to spend the rest of the trip with a piece of wood dangling on the bobstay, but it was preferable to being marooned with that moronic family.

Just as we were freed, Arthur, Dennis and Joan sailed past, jeering and waving so hard that they lost control and nearly rammed us. Joan was just visible as a pair of eyes over the cock-pit combing as she prepared hot toddies over the stove.

Beaver was furious. No sooner had the last sliver of wood parted than he commanded us to cast off and pursue 'that floating gin-palace'. The wind was as bad as ever and by the time we were well under way (after a couple of alarming false starts in which we nearly sailed into the bungalow again) the others had a good lead on us. We lost sight of them and then caught up on a nasty stretch where the bungalows and trees end and the wind can scream unhindered round a bend. *Quiet Dawn* was in the reeds, rocking wildly, while Dennis poked about with the quant pole. The sight cheered us up no end.

Our companion boat was the only craft we saw on the river as we tacked down towards Thurne Mouth in a wind that was rising, if that was possible, and in scuds of rain. We went into the reeds five times, took the jib off and went in again. By the time Thurne Dyke was reached even Beaver had had enough and it was agreed to moor there for the night.

Thurne Dyke is a pretty little backwater off the mainstream, about two hundred yards long. The scenery is typical: flat fields with black-and-white cattle grazing as far as the eye can see, windmills dotting the skyline and one particularly well-preserved mill by the dyke itself. When the fenland that formed the Broads was drained three hundred years ago the earth shrank until most of the fields were below the level of the rivers, so the Broads windmills were built for pumping water, not grinding corn. Although Thurne Mill stands by itself, many mills have a derelict steam pumping house next to them, and beside that a modern electric pumping station which has superseded the steam.

Normally, the fields appear to be full of white sails from the yachts on the rivers, but not on this occasion. *Merryweather II* and *Quiet Dawn* were alone.

The first time I sailed into Thurne Dyke, and that was some years previously, I went in at a spanking rate with the wind behind me, only to find that there wasn't room to turn round and come about into wind. We zoomed down the dyke, with the end looming nearer and nearer, our boom almost brushing moored boats, and no solution in sight. Then one of the crew remembered the mud-weight, a great block of metal which is the Broads equivalent of an anchor. It was a race against time to drag it from the forepeak and make it fast astern before dropping it when it put the brake on, so to speak. I have looked through the many books on yachting to find advice on a situation like this and there is none. They seem to concentrate on more esoteric problems, such as what to do if your rhumb line has a bend in it.

Beaver approached the dyke with unusual caution, took sail down at the entrance and had the boat walked along to a mooring. I made a mental note that he must have been getting old. *Quiet Dawn* arrived half an hour later. We had taken three hours to cover a stretch that would normally take one. This fact had not eluded Beaver, who spent the evening reshaping the schedule.

The last thing I remember before I dropped off to sleep was the wind shrieking outside, the rain pattering on the cabin roof and Beaver saying: 'Dawn start tomorrow. We've got to make Yarmouth by lunch.'

A COARSE SAILOR'S BEAUFORT SCALE

SPECIFICATION OF BEAUFORT SCALE

Beaufort number	Description of wind	For Coarse use, based on observations made at Potter Heigham and Bosham	For use on land, based on observations made at land stations	Speed in nautical m.p.h.
0	Calm	Boat moves sideways with tide	Cigarette smoke gets in eyes	Less than 1
1	Light air	Coarse yachtsmen hoist sail, then wind instantly drops	Wet finger feels cold	1–3
2	Light breeze	Coarse sailors keep on quanting or rowing	Public houses close one window	4–6
3	Gentle breeze	Coarse boats career. Difficult to make tea under way	Public houses close two windows	7–10
4	Moderate breeze	Coarse boats lose mainsheet through block and have to go aground to recover it	Beer froth blows off	11–16
5	Fresh breeze	Coarse sailors get book on sailing from cabin and turn up bit on reefing	Customers in public-house gardens go inside bar	17–21
6	Strong breeze	Coarse sailors try to double reef and go aground	Elderly customers have difficulty in leaving public house	22–27
7	Moderate gale	Coarse sailors rescued by launch	Public-house door cannot be opened against wind	28–33
8	Fresh gale	Aaaaaaaaah . . .	Public-house sign blows down	34–40
9	Strong gale	Coarse sailors in public house	Coarse sailors struck by falling sign	41–47

N.B.—Although the Beaufort Scale goes up to Force 12 it is felt unlikely that anything over Force 9 would interest Coarse sailors except on a television programme.

Five

ONCE more it was a disturbed night, this time due to Harry's snoring. It really was the most dreadful noise. My old car once made a similar sound shortly before expiring on Ealing Common. That was rather an interesting experience because the car simply dissolved. All the parts wore out at the same time and it disintegrated, swerved across the road and hit a tree. The headlights, which had not worked for six months, promptly blazed on and refused to go out. I remember the policeman asking me why I was wearing one trouser clip on the left leg while driving, and I explained shamefacedly that whenever the car went through a puddle a jet of water used to shoot up by the handbrake, so I had to take this precaution. He thought I was trying to be funny.

However, enough of the car. Yachtsmen, who find snoring a menace in the confined quarters of a cabin, have several ways of trying to stop snoring and we tried them all. Beaver had a pet theory that the best was to whisper gently but firmly, 'Stop snoring,' in the ear of the offender. This message would eventually penetrate the subconscious, he said, and the snoring would cease. So he knelt by Harry, looking rather as if he were praying by the side of a catafalque, and whispered gently at him. This had no effect and he gradually whispered louder and louder until eventually he was bellowing 'STOP SNORING!' at the top of his voice. Harry promptly woke up and asked what all the noise was about.

Ten minutes later, when we had all settled down, he was as bad as ever. I thought he would bring the mast down. I recalled that a sudden shock was supposed to stop snoring so I sprinkled a few drops of water on Harry's face. The snoring

rose to a nightmarish crescendo and then he woke up. This time we made him promise not to try to sleep until we were all asleep. Twice he fell asleep first and we woke him up and told him to wait, and then we all fell into deep slumber.

During the night I had a dream about my old ancestor Jem Green. I was sinking in a storm-tossed ketch when Jem appeared in a lifeboat, wearing an enormous set of Victorian oilskins, and called on me to jump. I tried to vault the boat's rail and I couldn't. Lead weights were tied to my feet. Just as the boat foundered, Jem gave a great shout and I woke up. Then I became aware that the noise was still going on.

It took a few moments for me to orientate myself (I don't mean I pointed east, I mean to find where I was). When fully conscious I realized the noise was coming from Beaver, who was sitting bolt upright in his bunk with his arms outstretched and his eyes tightly closed and shouting his head off. He was calling out, 'Jump for it . . . Jump for it . . .' and then lapsing into a direful burble. Finally he gave a great shout, fell back on his bunk and slept like a babe.

The noise had awoken Arthur, who loves to spend the night wandering abroad, and he arrived, clumping about in heavy boots and thoroughly disturbing everyone. He nodded sagely when we told him what had happened and recalled that before the war, when he and Beaver had gone sailing, they had moored over a submerged stake which went straight through the bottom of the boat as the tide fell. They awoke in the middle of the night to find water lapping all round. Beaver had made a gallant effort to salvage something and was still in the cabin when the boat gave its final lurch. He swam out clutching a toothbrush. Ever since he had been subject to nightmares while afloat.

The only person undisturbed by all the commotion was Beaver himself, whose heavy breathing showed that he, at least, was having a good night.

We awoke at seven-thirty to a glorious, sunny morning. The storm had blown itself out and for the first time I felt I was on holiday. I even got up first, it being my turn to make the early-morning tea. By an extraordinary coincidence Joan was also making the early tea on *Quiet Dawn*.

When I took Beaver his cup he demanded to know what all the row had been about in the middle of the night. He complained that he had been awakened by me and Arthur arguing about something. Told he was the centre of the commotion, he refused to believe it.

'Nonsense,' he said. 'I was asleep all the time until you woke me up.'

He lowered his voice confidentially.

'Actually, old man, I reckon it was Sheila who disturbed you. These preggers women get strange fancies, y'know. I've been watching her closely. She's got that faraway look in her eyes. I wouldn't trust her on the helm like that.'

By nine o'clock we were on the move. A good number of fishermen were out and our progress was marked by various explosions along the bank. Anglers cannot for the life of them see why a yacht has to zig-zag along the river, snapping their lines or causing them to reel in violently. Unfortunately, there is rarely time to explain the theory of sailing.

I once sailed with an angling enthusiast. We tacked along a narrow channel down the centre of the river in our efforts to avoid anglers, with the result that we kept losing way and paying off into the reeds. When this happened my friend would be full of angling gossip, calling out: 'How are you doing? I presume you're legering with an Arlesey Bomb and a piece of herring,' or some such nonsense.

'I was,' replied the fisherman, 'but now my ruddy line's round the front of your boat.'

I'm afraid we were a bit of a nuisance in other ways that morning, principally to motor-cruisers. Broads cruisers are often far too big and powerful for those confined and crowded waterways and their size should be regulated. When you have three of these monsters trying to pass through several yachts tacking close together, it's no wonder trouble occurs. Most cruiser skippers like a signal from the yacht as to where they should pass, but the yachtsman often hasn't time, or in light airs just doesn't know. And, of course, there are plenty of cruiser helmsmen who don't understand why a yacht is zig-zagging and try to plough on under the fond impression that the yacht can stop, as they can.

Then there is always the gentleman who isn't going to give way to anyone and who just roars straight ahead.

The most dangerous type of all, though, is the car-driver sailor, he who parks his motor-cruiser by reversing to and fro as if in a London square. Last year one of them actually reversed across the river at Yarmouth and held up his hand to me to stop. As the alternative to hitting him was to go on to the mud, probably for eight hours, I rammed him amidships.

On the whole, though, nearly all cruiser people try to appreciate a yacht's difficulties and many a yacht has been grateful for a kindly tow off the mud, even though cruisers are not supposed to do this. But for the life of me I can't find an excuse for the angler, unless he wants to sleep.

Beaver handed over the tiller for a time and vanished below while I took over. Even when Beaver gives up the helm one never feels one is really in command. At times of minor crisis he is liable to seize it from your grasp and blame you for the subsequent collision. This time I was just congratulating myself that I had the boat on my own for a few minutes when the hatch over the lavatory opened, and Beaver stuck his head out and shouted: 'Stop pinching her. Put your helm up a bit.'

Having discovered this novel position of command, Beaver was in high glee, and he spent a full half-hour sitting there distributing orders.

At Acle Bridge, *Quiet Dawn*, which was ahead, stopped to take down the mast to pass under the bridge. To gain an advantage Beaver decided to shoot the bridge, i.e. take the mast down under way, glide through and raise the mast on the other side in midstream.

The mast on a Broads boat is pivoted with a heavy weight at the bottom. In theory it is easy enough to raise or lower, taking the strain on the forestay, but in practice the effect of the forestay is lost as the mast becomes nearly horizontal and you have to be careful the mast doesn't crash down.

All went suspiciously well at first. We took sail off and about a hundred yards from the bridge Harry grasped the forestay, and I kept both feet firmly planted on the counterweight at the bottom of the mast as an additional precaution against accidents while Beaver tugged gently at the mast to start it moving. It had just started to come down when a motor-cruiser passed us flat out and the wash knocked Harry off his feet. Beaver lost his balance as well, and instinctively clung to the mast for support, which merely pulled it down faster. The only things exerting force in the other direction were the weight at the bottom of the mast and me standing on it.

Sometime I should like an engineer to work out the exact forces to which I was subjected in terms of foot pounds per square inch as the mast came down. They would probably be sufficient to do something unlikely, such as lift two dozen eggs a distance of three hundred feet. Anyway, they were powerful enough to hurl me upwards and outwards. I had a fleeting glimpse of Harry's startled face on the deck beneath and then I was four feet under the River Bure. I recall being surprised at how salty the water was, considering we were a dozen miles from the sea.

I have a horror of coming up underneath a boat so I swam lustily under water while my trousers ballooned about me with the air trapped inside before becoming soaked and pulling me down like lead weights. As usual on these occasions, I was swimming in the wrong direction and I surfaced just by the stern. From what I could see, unhappy though my predicament was, I was well out of things by being overboard. The tiller swung unattended as Sheila, who had been on the helm, sat helpless in a cocoon of ropes and rigging (heaven knows why the mast didn't hit her on the head). Beaver lay apparently lifeless on the cabin-top. Harry was kicking feebly at the wreckage.

As I hauled myself inboard, Beaver raised his head and said, 'Good God, what happened?'

A familiar voice called from the bank. 'Boyur,' came the rustic accents of Arthur, 'yew got that there mast down a bit quick, didn't yew?'

In fact, despite the chaos, we had achieved what we set out to do and were now drifting through the bridge in a haphazard fashion, watched by the inevitable crowd of bloodthirsty ghouls. The simplest way of clearing the mess was to raise the mast again, but it had to be done quickly. One doesn't drift around sideways near Acle Bridge for long without someone hitting you.

Harry heaved on the forestay, I stood on the counterweight again and Beaver lifted from the cabin-top. The mast groaned up a few inches and then stuck as the shrouds caught the corners of the cabin. Beaver got them free, called for a mighty effort, and we all heaved. This time we were stopped by a shrill scream from Sheila, who under Beaver's strict instructions had been sitting passive under the tangled rigging, not daring to move in case she made matters worse.

A rope had somehow wound itself round her ankle and she was being dragged upside down up the mast. I have never seen a woman being dragged upside down up a mast before, and I must say that the spectacle was most interesting. In fact if it hadn't been for the others I would have seen if we could have got her to the top.

Eventually the mast swung upright, the base thumped into the socket and I rammed home the piece of metal which secured it.

'Hoist sail,' shouted Beaver.

This was easier said than done. All the ropes had tied themselves into obscure knots that would have taken hours to tie deliberately (why is it that left to its own devices a rope ties a knot much more complicated than anyone could invent?). I was just trying to unravel the jib halyard when Beaver called, 'Stand by to fend off.' We were drifting gently into a motorized wherry moored by the bank.

We struck the wherry a soft glancing blow. A red-faced man in a blue jersey appeared and created as much fuss as if we had rammed her at full speed, demanding why we came 'down here' barging all over the river and scraping people's paint.

I notice that this type of person always makes his criticisms from a vessel fitted with a nice twenty-horsepower engine. I have never met one actually sailing. It is one thing to shout at people in yachts and wear a blue jersey and look professional and quite another to sail a yacht yourself. Yachtsmen themselves rarely abuse each other (unless racing, of course). Not that one wishes to castigate professional watermen. Most of them are kindly, friendly experts, like the one we met years ago

sailing a converted wherry on the Yare. Despite the fact that
the wherry is only a superior sailing barge, he challenged us to
a race and won hands down. Then he started his auxiliary
engine and gave us a tow all the way to Brundall. A real
gent.

The worst of this little incident was that while we were
hoisting sail we had scarcely any way and had to put up with
a stream of abuse for almost five minutes. But Beaver has rather
a good turn of wit on occasions and when the man stopped for
breath he said sweetly: 'Do you mind repeating all that? I'm
afraid I'm deaf.'

The contretemps cost us our lead over Arthur, who tacked
past as we hoisted sail. There followed a grim battle in which
Beaver not only broke all the rules of sailing but produced a few
of his own as we jockeyed for position ('Give way, Arthur, can't
you see I'm fore-reaching'). This passed the time pleasantly
enough until we came to the little riverside village of Stokesby,
two miles downstream, and Beaver having managed to get his
nose in front shouted to Arthur that we ought to stop for a
drink.

Arthur agreed and started to manœuvre *Quiet Dawn* to the
bank. And then an astonishing thing happened. As he came
alongside he passed close to a motor-cruiser going in the
opposite direction and Dennis's cat, which had been mewing
piteously in the bows, leaped on to the other boat.

It was all over in a moment and I was the only one who
noticed. I shouted to the cruiser and to Arthur, but the cruiser
was speeding out of earshot and by the time Arthur and Dennis
understood what I was saying he was past the bend and
heading for Acle at six knots with the cat washing itself on the
stern.

There was only one thing that could be done. Arthur swung
Quiet Dawn round, and with the wind behind him headed for-
lornly upstream after the cruiser, Dennis in the bows shouting
loudly, 'You've got our cat on board, give us back our pussy.'

They, too, disappeared round the bend. The sun shone and
all was silent except for the lapping of water and the diminish-
ing banshee howls of 'Pussy, Pussy' in the distance. We went
for a midday pint with great peace in our hearts.

Rolling Down to Burnham

(A sea shanty)

Oh, sitting in the yacht club
A-listening to the wind
I spied a pretty maiden
A-drinking it-and-gin.

> Chorus: With a rifo, rifo, stick it up the mast-oh,
> Away, away, look away.

Oh she did look so pretty
In her sweater chunky knit
That I upped me anchor straight away
And by her I did sit.

> Chorus: With a rifo, rifo, stick it, etc., etc.

Oh maiden, maiden, maiden,
When will you marry me?
Alas, alas, I cannot,
Actually I'm engaged to a rather nice chap who
works for an oil firm.

> Chorus: With a rifo, rifo, etc., etc.

Rolling Down to Burnham

Words by Michael Green

Music by Guy Eldridge

Robust and rollicking

1. Oh, sitt-ing in the yacht club
2. Oh, she did look so pretty In her

1. listening to the wind I spied a pretty maid-en A-
2. sweater chunky knit That I upped me anchor straight a-way And

f Chorus

1. drinking it-and-gin With a ri-fo, ri-fo, stick it up the mast-oh
2. by her I did sit.

ff

A-way, a-way, look a-way.

Six

LUNCH was slightly farcical. Sheila cooked some spaghetti which stuck to the bottom of the pot (a fortune awaits the man who will invent non-glutinous spaghetti) and we amused ourselves by smothering it in sauces and outrageous condiments. To our great surprise *Quiet Dawn* hove into view before the meal was finished and moored at the staithe. At first we couldn't see the cat, and then Harry spotted it peering out of a cabin port-hole with an expression which quite plainly indicated it was planning further mischief.

Dennis carried Pussy over and told us what had happened. Apparently the cruiser skipper had gone only a few hundred yards when the cat jumped on to the back of his neck. The shock was so great that he drove the boat into the bank, swearing never to touch another drop. Pussy then defied all efforts to catch him and led the man and his wife in a fantastic chase all over the boat. When Dennis sailed by chanting 'Pussy, Pussy' they hailed him with positive gratitude and almost offered to pay him to take the animal away.

Of course we all made a great fuss of the cat, which thanked us by eating a tin of sardines and climbing up the rigging, where it defied all efforts at rescue for half an hour. Finally we had to lower the wretched mast again.

Beaver chafed at the delay and as soon as the cat was rescued we set sail. From Stokesby onwards the River Bure rolls pleasantly through low-lying pastures for about three miles until the Stracey Arms Hotel is reached. After that, as one nears the estuary at Yarmouth, the river becomes foul, muddy, evil and treacherous, a trap for unwary yachts with its shoals, mudbanks and swirling currents. At low tide the navigable channel is reduced to a few feet in places.

The weather changed in sympathy as we sailed past Stracey Arms. Dark clouds obscured the sun and a chill breeze sprang up. It was against us, of course. The wind is always against you when sailing, unless for some reason you want it that way, in which case it veers round and blows from astern. I remember sailing in Chichester harbour and tacking down to Hayling Island against a stiff breeze. When we turned to go back to Itchenor the wind promptly changed so it was against us, and then dropped away to a mere puff. The result was that the tide turned long before we were home. Then a dreadful thing happened. One of the crew tapped me on the shoulder and said, 'Land is springing up all round us.'

He was right too. As the tide raced out stretches of land were actually marching towards the boat faster than we could sail away. In fact the land caught us up and we grounded. It was dark when we were towed back.

Beaver hated this stretch of the Bure, or the Cruel Bure as he called it. He hated it as if it were alive, swearing that when the river greedily swirled at the muddy banks he could hear it chuckle at him, mocking his efforts.

We were going down on the ebb, so if we went aground we would have to act quickly or otherwise we should be in trouble. There is only one certain way of getting off Broads mud, if the quant pole sinks in futilely, and that is to jump overboard and push. There would be fewer spoiled holidays if more people did this instead of wringing their hands and waiting for a tow.

The mud looks unpleasant but it rarely comes higher than your hips and it doesn't smell too bad as long as you don't breathe deeply. Also, it is quite warm.

It is, of course, necessary to exercise some care when jumping overboard. I once bounded over the side when we went aground in Holland, having carefully changed into my bathing costume, and found the water was only a foot deep. The bottom was shingle and I sprained my ankle. This, mind you, was in the middle of a lake. I felt an absolute fool.

Quiet Dawn was the first to go aground. Arthur and Dennis don't like going overboard unless it's absolutely necessary and they spent a long time poking with the quant without success, so we tacked past and a quarter of a mile further on we went aground too. The bottom was so soft that the quant made little impression. Harry jumped overboard and pushed in two feet of water and two feet of mud. Nothing happened. I hopped over and we both pushed and this time *Merryweather* slid off. Beaver was anxious to beat Arthur to Yarmouth and was going too near the bank on his tacks, so two minutes later he went aground again. Harry and I went over and this time Arthur passed us as we floundered in the mud.

We pushed the bow round and *Merryweather* went across on the other tack. 'Ready about,' said Beaver optimistically, as we neared the bank, and then we slid to a standstill. We were stuck again.

Anyone listening would have heard the sound of loud voices raised in anger followed by a heavy splash as a fat, bearded, middle-aged man went overboard.

After that Beaver did not go aground again.

We overtook Arthur fast aground on a notorious shoal just by the Smith's Potato Crisp factory at Yarmouth. Arthur must love that shoal. At any rate he spends half an hour there every year. On one occasion he spent the night fast aground on the mud. To stop the boat heeling over as the tide ran out he swung the boom ashore and pinned it to the ground with a rond anchor, a real Coarse Sailing wheeze if ever there was one.

Another method of keeping the boat upright in a similar crisis is to plunge the quant pole into the mud as a prop. It is most important not to let the boat heel over, because when the tide starts making she may stay fixed in the mud and start to fill. A year or two ago we passed a young couple fast aground and heard them say, 'Well, we may as well stay here the night.' They answered our warnings with pitying smiles (Beaver may have been a little rude, of course) but, sure enough, next day we saw them standing miserably on the bank with the boat half full of muddy water.

Once again I have looked through my sailing books for useful tips such as those outlined above and have failed to find them. There are whole chapters on what sort of schooner to buy and how to reef the mizzen in a hurricane, even the correct procedure to adopt when landing in a foreign country ('Be sure to fly international flag Q, meaning "My vessel is

healthy and I require free *pratique*" '), but nothing on what
to do when hopelessly stuck on the mud by some dolt.

I suppose, of course, one could fly a flag of distress when
aground, but nobody seems to pay attention to them. My
friend on the Hamble has a lovely collection ranging from 'I
Am Discharging Explosives' to 'You Should Stop, I Have
Something Important to Communicate to You'.

Well, one fine Saturday we went aground in Southampton
Water and having nothing better to do we flew international
flag F, meaning 'I am disabled. Communicate with me.' Boats
came and went. Some passed quite near. Quite a few exchanged
greetings. But nobody knew what the flag meant. Eventually we
flew our ensign upside down as well and when that didn't work
we flew flag O, meaning 'Man overboard', and still nobody
bothered about us, although the *Queen Mary* passed only a mile
away on her way to Southampton and you'd think somebody
on a boat that size would know what flags mean.

As a last resort we let off a miserable little flare which my
friend had kept for thirteen years, waiting for the ultimate
emergency, and all that happened was that the boat was filled
with smoke and a man passing in a motor-boat said, 'A bit
early for fireworks, isn't it?'

Heaven knows what would have happened if we had been
really in trouble. As it was, we waited for the tide in disgust
and floated off. But as we were mooring some officious chap
rowed by in a dinghy and commented, 'I say, you've got your
ensign upside down.' Fool.

Yarmouth, which we were now approaching, is the supreme
test of Broads sailing. The tide swirls viciously past the yacht
station, immediately beyond which are three low bridges waiting to catch your mast. To make matters worse a high jetty and
some houses take away the wind, while opposite is a treacherous
shoal.

It is a standing amusement for the locals to come down to
the yacht station on a summer's evening and watch the boats
coming alongside. They come, not to see the graceful shapes
gliding into the jetty, but to hear the howls of dismay and fear
as the aforesaid graceful shapes are dashed against the railway
bridge with a snapping of timber. They are rarely disappointed.

Sunday evening is the best time, for Yarmouth is like a bottleneck between the northern and southern sections of the Broads and it is then all the yachts crowd in, ready to start on the morning tide. This week Sunday's storms had delayed everyone by a day and Monday evening was the busy one. The jetty was crowded as we rounded the corner and the wind, which had hitherto been persistently against us, immediately began to blow towards the jetty in fitful gusts.

However, Beaver knows Yarmouth. There are all sorts of theoretical things to do, but the golden rule is to come alongside as soon as possible. He came about and ghosted back diagonally across the stream with a slack mainsheet and the tide taking off most of our way, and as we came near the jetty Harry nimbly hopped from the bows with a line on to a moored boat and made us fast temporarily round its shrouds.

Somehow I don't think this method would be approved by the Royal Yacht Squadron, but it worked.

As soon as sail was down we climbed up on to the jetty to join the ghouls watching the other yachts come in. I wouldn't miss the sight for anything. It's my annual treat, the thought of which sustains me through the long winter months. The first boat to come down was a Bermudan-rigged sloop with a honeymoon couple on board. At least I didn't know for sure, but they must have been honeymooners because every other word was 'Darling'.

As they came round the bend the husband said, 'Darling, would you go forward and get out the mud-weight, darling?'

His bride walked to the bows and stood looking helplessly.

'Where is it, darling?'

'In the forepeak, darling. Under the hatch, dearest.'

Under a beam wind and a four-knot tide they sped towards the first bridge.

'Can you find the weight, darling? It's rather urgent, sweetheart.'

'Yes, I'm looking, darling, but there's a lot of luggage on top of it, dear.'

The husband looked apprehensively at the bridge.

'Oh, do hurry, darling. We shall hit the bridge.'

'I *am* hurrying, darling. You'll just have to slow the boat down.'

A pause. Then:

'Darling, for God's sake get out that blasted mud-weight and stop mucking about.'

The woman looked up, burst into tears and cried: 'Oh, get your own stupid mud-weight, darling. I'm sick of you and sick of this boat and sick of this rotten holiday. I *hate* it.'

The bridge was about ten yards away. With commendable presence of mind the husband swung the boat round and plunged into the mud on the right bank of the river. He then started a slanging match with his bride, in the course of which I learned a lot of interesting things about their respective family histories, including the fact that the bride wished she had married a bloke called Julian. It was so interesting that all the watchers applauded.

A man who stopped his yacht by the remarkable expedient of scraping alongside all the moored craft was next and he was followed by Arthur. Yarmouth is Arthur's *bête noir*. He's never yet got in without being the centre of an admiring crowd, and his fans were not disappointed this time.

With a great shout of 'Boyur' *Quiet Dawn* turned into wind in the middle of the river for no apparent reason and started to drift sideways towards the railway bridge at an alarming rate. Dennis poked the quant pole into the water tentatively and could not touch bottom. The jib had been dropped and the boat wouldn't pay off. Joan had been given her post of danger by the boom crutches and she stood clutching them and staring wide-eyed at the fast-approaching bridge.

Advice was hurled at them from all sides, as always. Beaver bellowed for Arthur to hoist his jib and get some way on. A group of locals called out for him to drop his mud-weight while a beery-looking individual told him to start his engine. Meanwhile Dennis was trying to restore steerage way by rowing with the quant pressed against the mast, looking rather like an ancient Phoenician oarsman. Arthur was waggling the tiller with some intention which could not be determined.

When it seemed they must hit the bridge the yacht-station attendant arrived, scenting trouble, and hurled them a long line.

Nobody paid any attention to it. Dennis was still prodding

. . . *landed on Arthur's head*

the river as if he expected to find gold there, Arthur was shouting and gesticulating and Joan was holding the crutches as if her life depended on it.

'Tell the missy not to bother about them crutches and to take hold of the line,' shouted the waterman.

Joan reached out a tentative hand and missed it. The waterman hauled it in and threw again. This time it landed on Arthur's head and he clutched it gratefully. (They were so near the bridge that Dennis was using the Broadsman's last resort—fending the boat off with the quant pole on the bridge girders. But you can't keep it up for more than a few minutes, your arm muscles become tired and you're doomed.)

A group of ghouls heaved on the rope and drew Arthur to safety.

'Not bad,' muttered Beaver. 'Usually Arthur manages to sink someone.' As he spoke there was a splash and Joan fell overboard, still holding the crutches and rolling her eyes.

We fished her out from the deck of a motor-cruiser the other side of the railway bridge, where the tide carried her. A woman on the cruiser, a motherly, middle-aged Northerner, was appalled as we dragged the poor girl from the water like a sack of potatoes, having first salvaged the crutches.

'Ee, you poor lass,' she said. 'Why do you do it?'

'Oh, we don't mind,' squeaked Joan bravely, rubbing the diesel oil from her face. 'It's *fun* to us.'

Seven

NEXT morning I blew the boat up.

Like so many of the world's great events it happened quite casually, almost in passing, as it were. I got up early to make tea, as we planned to go through the three bridges on the last of the ebb. It was not my turn, but late the previous evening the boat was found to be in peril of drifting away, thanks to the way I had tied up, and this was a penance. The time was just after six o'clock on a dull, drizzly morning, quite a contrast to the previous day. It had been a peaceful night as we were all too tired to bother about Harry's snoring, although Arthur disturbed us by tramping round the deck in the middle of the night warning us that the tide fell nine feet, as if we didn't know.

I opened the lid of the cooking locker, turned on the gas, struck a match and was enveloped in a sheet of flame. Out of sheer self-preservation I instantly jumped overboard. I swear I *hissed* as I touched the water.

The tide carried me away and I was fifty yards downstream before I managed to grasp the stern of a motor-cruiser moored by the jetty. The occupants had a shock when a white, shrivelled and dripping hand was thrust through a port-hole as I clambered aboard. I heard a little gasp from a bunk immediately underneath, but I was past caring.

When I walked back to the boat they were all looking over the side and debating as to whether I could still be alive. This callous attitude appalled me. You get to know your friends on a trip like this. Beaver was actually saying, 'He must have gone down like a stone, we'll have to call out the police frogmen,' when I placed my hand on his shoulder and said 'Beaver' in

. . . I instantly jumped overboard

sepulchral tones. He turned and went quite pale. Apparently I was dripping wet and minus one eyebrow, which gave me a slightly quizzical appearance.

Beaver, after recovering, accused me of leaving the Calor gas turned on at the main all night, which I considered most unfeeling of him, although it was quite true. His chief concern was whether the boat was damaged. Since the explosion had felt like a bomb going off I was surprised to find it wasn't, and this rather weakened my story that I had been blown through the air for fifty yards, surviving only because of an iron constitution.

I claimed a glass of brandy from Beaver's private stock, which he always referred to as 'the medicinal stores', and had breakfast on my bunk, while Arthur regaled me with some yarn about a barrage balloon exploding in the war and how everyone thought they were all right and then they all dropped dead three days later from delayed shock. I warned him that if I had any more of that he might get an undelayed shock.

I couldn't rest long because we had to take down the mast and shoot the bridges. Everyone else was doing the same and there was a rare old cluster of boats going through. There were boats going backwards, boats going sideways, boats going forwards and boats just stationary on the mud.

The official method of going through the Yarmouth bridges is to drop the mud-weight over the bows and drift down backwards with the tide, controlling your speed by letting the mud-weight brush the bottom. It is an incredible business and I have never known anyone achieve it successfully. We always rely on a good quant for steerage way, but one needs to know the bottom well, because in some places the river is too deep to quant while a few feet further on you're liable to go aground. If the tide is running fast, we keep the mud-weight handy on the stern as a precaution. One year Arthur found himself going too fast and threw the weight overboard to check the boat. He then discovered he had forgotten to tie the weight to anything and it sank with a mocking gurgle, lost for ever.

As usual, some fool in a motor-cruiser tried to pass all the yachts like a Jaguar overtaking a line of lorries, and his wash caused chaos and confusion. To add insult to injury he was actually cursing as he drove by. People like this should be made to quant a yacht while someone drives past at eight knots. After falling overboard a couple of times they might be more careful.

After passing the third bridge both boats moored at the coal wharf (although how it got its name is a mystery, as they never seem to unload coal there). The only alternative is to moor at the dolphins provided for yachts, but it is no use doing this for the simple reason that they are built on shoal and you will certainly go aground if you moor on the first two at low water. A brilliant piece of marine engineering.

The coal wharf is an old stamping ground of ours. Often we have spent the night there after shooting the bridges at dusk. It was here Dennis walked straight off the jetty into the river on a pitch-black night and here that just after the war Beaver sprained his ankle tripping over a heap of old iron and crawled painfully back to the boat calling for help.

The official tugman has his mooring near here, situated strategically at the junction of the Bure and the Yare, and makes a healthy living by pulling boats off the mud. He is a busy man, for the tides are strong and treacherous and the notorious Breydon Water, a four-mile stretch of mud partly covered in water, lies just ahead.

The first time we employed his services was when we went aground in a gale between Yarmouth and Stracey Arms, and our boom was broken when Arthur tried to sail alongside and tow us off. Arthur took back our S O S and out came the tugman in his powerful launch, with his dog sitting in the bows (it died some years later and we all felt we had lost a friend). It took a long time to salvage us, for we were firmly fixed, but eventually he managed it and towed us back to Yarmouth. Not having used his services before, we debated on the way whether to tip him or not, and decided to give him twenty cigarettes.

I leaned over the side when we tied up and said: 'Thanks very much, that was very decent of you. Here's something for your trouble.'

He took the cigarettes and handed me a bill for thirty-two-and-sixpence salvage charges.

'And you be lucky,' he said. 'I charge a pound a tide usually, and extra for pulling 'em off Breydon.'

After that we nicknamed him Sinbad. He got to know us so well in later years that sometimes he would give us a free tow, saying slyly, 'I won't let your pals know you was stuck.'

By some freak of nature the tide starts to make up the Yare an hour earlier than on the Bure, so as soon as the mast was raised and sail set we cast off, and with one gigantic heave from the quant pole to get under way we were at the junction of the two rivers. To the left lay Yarmouth harbour and the sea, but hired boats are forbidden to enter the harbour and our course was to turn right, into the Yare, and sail inland.

The Yare is an important commercial river, in the old days a great wherry highway, and still much used by ocean vessels steaming up to Norwich. It is unusual in that its estuary is now inland and has become Breydon Water. There is a dredged channel in the middle about a hundred yards wide and desolate mud-flats beyond this, covered at high tide. It is typical of the stupid River Yare that having formed a nice estuary over the centuries it should go on piling up so much mud that the estuary became land-locked and now Breydon Water is separated from the sea by a strip of land and the river goes on to join the Bure and a new estuary outside Yarmouth. They built Yarmouth on the mud it piled up.

Beaver was chafing to get on, and we left *Quiet Dawn* behind, stuck on the mud. When we last saw them Arthur and Dennis were arguing as to who should jump overboard and push her off. The first hazard on entering the Yare is a railway swing bridge, now fixed, but with nasty currents between the arches. The wind being fitful we drifted through the left-hand arch and were promptly seized by The Giant Hand. This is the name Dennis gave to a strange current just past the bridge which has a habit of seizing yachts without much way and casting them ashore. The wind dropped completely for a moment, as it frequently does in those parts, and we were carried firmly to the mud at the edge of Breydon. Beaver cursed, shouted, swore at the wind and the crew, but without result. We grounded firmly on the desolate shore.

'Go over, Harry,' commanded Beaver, when my poking with the quant produced no effect in the soft mud.

The water at the bows was only about six inches deep so

Harry took off his shoes and plunged over quite happily. Next moment he rose vertically in the air as if propelled upwards by an underwater spring, and delivered a loud howl.

It appeared he had jumped straight on to a piece of broken glass. At first we thought he had lost a foot at least, because he cried, 'Don't let Sheila see it, she might lose the baby.' Naturally this only made Sheila more anxious to speak with him before he expired, but Harry continued to lie on the foredeck, writhing round and round clutching his foot and crying: 'Don't look. It's the blood.'

I went for'd gingerly and was permitted to examine the wound, which was a minute cut about half an inch long. Harry said it felt about six inches long and he was sure I hadn't found the real wound. I told him to look for himself and he spent several minutes peering curiously at his foot and getting his hands covered in blood which he wiped on the jib, so that the boat looked as if a gang of pirates had attacked us.

Beaver's contribution was to remark: 'The water's filthy, you know. I bet it's riddled with sewage and all sorts of muck. You want to watch out for tetanus, Harry. I'm glad *I* haven't cut myself, that's all.'

Meanwhile Arthur sailed by, hailing us with some sarcastic remark about it not being a very nice place for a picnic. Arthur can be a little jarring at times. I could see Joan bending over the cooking locker, doubtless engaged in some expensive fricassee.

While Harry's wound was being washed, I pushed the bows off and we sailed away. Sinbad overtook us and exchanged greetings, saying he was going to make his third attempt to rescue a motor-cruiser which had gone aground two days previously on the highest tide for six months. Later we passed the vessel, its occupants looking very sorry for themselves as Sinbad described endless figures-of-eight round them. They were at least fifty yards outside the marked channel, so we presumed they were trying to take a short cut, not realizing the importance of those silly black and red posts.

The wind freshened considerably as we came nearer to the centre of Breydon, and Beaver decided we should reef, as the boat was becoming difficult to handle.

Reefing under way, as described in the textbooks, is, of course, simplicity itself. The instructions usually run something like this:

'Now we must prepare for foul weather. Let us assume that the wind has risen to gale force and the boat is threatening to capsize. First, keep calm and do not run for harbour. Remember that drowning is not an unpleasant death whereas if you get on a lee shore you may be dashed to pieces against the rocks. Next take in a reef, or two if you feel like it. Head the boat into wind, nip smartly for'd and lower the jib, haul up the topping lift to take the weight off the sail, lower the gaff so that the cringle on the luff can be tied to the boom, roll up the leech between the first reef cringle and the clew, place it on top of the boom, tie the leech cringle to the boom, then roll up the sail carefully and tie in the reef points, and in a trice you are snugly reefed.'

Hmmm. . . .
I think I could just manage all that in the middle of a perfectly calm sea with no other craft in sight and all day to do it. My experience is that even when moored securely I have never reefed in under an hour and then I usually find I've tied something wrong somewhere and have to start all over again. The thought of drifting helplessly about Breydon Water out of control for two hours at nine-thirty in the morning doesn't bear thinking about.

Our experience this time bore out my impression. Beaver rounded up in the middle of the channel, and we took the jib down all right, and scandalized the mainsail. But by then we were drifting broadside on across the main channel, up which a large public pleasure cruiser, named *Pride of the Broads*, was proceeding. I pointed this out to Beaver, who merely said we would have to be quick with the reefing, that was all. Well, I never was much good at knots and things, and by the time Harry and I had got that bit about the cringle done (I never really know what a cringle is, it sounds like a word meaning 'to slink away'), *Pride of the Broads* was looming over us, loudspeakers playing music and its siren hooting.

'Move over . . . !'

Theoretically, of course, power craft give way to sail, but there is a little rhyme about

> 'Here lies the body of Harold Day
> Who insisted on his right of way.'

Beaver, however, shouted: 'Move over, you bloody great steam-kettle, can't you see I'm out of command? Give way, can't you?'

The *Pride of the Broads* replied by passing within two feet of us, so that Sheila squeaked with fright. The passengers peered down curiously from the deck above and one small boy spat on us (he missed, I'm glad to say). Beaver voided himself of two Anglo-Saxon words and was rewarded by a jeering toot.

As we were now drifting towards the mud, Harry and I untied our one miserable, pathetic knot and hoisted sail again. I don't think Beaver noticed. He was still shaking his fist at the pleasure boat and swearing while a group of elderly people sitting in the stern nodded, smiled and waved at him.

Later, when we mentioned the incident to Arthur, he said we should have hoisted two black balls to show we were not under command. As if we were likely to find two black balls anywhere. In fact, I made up a rhyme:

> 'Here lies the body of Harold Halls
> Who forgot to hoist up two black balls.'

We came to the end of Breydon Water at ten-thirty. Here there is another fork where the River Waveney runs into the Yare. It's a lonely, desolate spot—the loneliest in the world on a dark, drizzling night when one is trying to reach Yarmouth— but upstream lies some very pleasant country on both rivers, although they are rather treacherous for a mile or two. Our route took us up the Yare to Reedham, where according to schedule we were due to lunch. The tide was flooding strongly so we had no trouble with the mud and we reached Reedham in splendid time, helped by a spanking breeze, mostly on the beam.

The river bends sharply to the right just before Reedham,

where the New Cut joins it, and the approach to the village itself is guarded by a railway swing bridge. Like all Broads swing bridges this will open to let yachts and other tall craft through, but its normal position is closed. If a train is coming the signalman, provided he remembers, hangs out a board with a figure 5 or 10 to signify the number of minutes craft must wait.

The bridge was open as we came round the bend, and very pretty it looked in its white paint. It had an odd air of Victorian gracefulness. Beaver sprinted for the gap, if one can say that of a yacht. Through turning, however, the wind was against us and partly blanketed by the bridge, so we didn't approach it very swiftly. When we were a few yards away the signalman opened the window of his box, shouted a warning and started to close the bridge.

We had an interesting choice of having the mast caught as the bridge swung; trying to tack through the gap before the bridge closed; or retreating. Beaver, as might be expected, decided to try to beat the bridge. There was one moment of sheer horror when we all saw he wouldn't make it, but the relief was glorious when the wind died completely under the bridge and we drifted into some piling beside it. Harry hopped on to the piling and towed us back as the bridge clanged to, just missing our shrouds.

We waited a few minutes and a train passed over but the bridge didn't open. A further ten minutes and Arthur's mast appeared round the corner and Beaver began to get mad.

He cast off from the piling and sailed up and down in front of the bridge, shouting 'Bridge ahoy' as if it were a ship. We all felt the need for one for those little trumpets which Dutch boats use in similar circumstances. This produces a noise like a dying frog, and when the bridge controller hears the unmistakable sound he opens the bridge. I have known it to fail only once in Holland, and on that occasion we sailed up and down blowing for a quarter of an hour before a man in baggy trousers and clogs told us by signs that the canal was now closed. This was great news, because it meant we had just travelled twenty miles to no purpose.

One reason why the Dutch bridges open so readily is the

charming tradition in which the bridge operator hangs out a clog on a sort of fishing-line and you drop money into it as you pass. If you fail to drop in any money you will find all the other bridges mysteriously closed to your boat. The first time this happened none of us knew why the man was dangling this dirty old clog so ostentatiously, so we just smiled and waved and I thought he was offering the clog as a souvenir and actually grabbed it as we went past.

Like most Dutch canals, this one went through the centre of the village and we couldn't understand why two or three people ran along the quayside after us, waving their arms and hurling abuse. It was most unlike the friendly Dutch. Finally we gathered we had done something wrong, and turned back. It all ended happily. We gave the man back his clog and his fee, and he informed us that we were flying the Dutch flag upside down, which solved another mystery, namely why so many people had shouted at us throughout the trip.

After a time the signalman came and looked out of his window and gazed down at us, smoking a contented pipe. He was obviously a person at peace with the world. Not so Beaver. When Arthur drew level and tacked to and fro his fury knew no bounds, especially when Arthur, who is a railway maniac, said he was rather pleased to have the chance of seeing a train as it went over the bridge.

'If you ask me,' Arthur called over the water, 'he's waiting for the eleven-eighteen up mail from Lowestoft to clear that there crossover near Somerleyton.'

'If you ask me,' retorted Beaver, 'he's a miserable old cross-over himself, and I'm going to have words with him.'

I was on the helm at the time and Beaver ordered me to put *Merryweather* into the reeds by the bank. It took about five minutes to scramble across the field and up the railway embankment to where the signalman was watching us benignly.

He showed no emotion until Beaver bounded up the steps of his box, flung open the door, and demanded: 'What the hell is going on? Why won't you open the bridge?'

No one had ever done this before, not even the captains of ocean-going steamers which use the Yare, and he didn't quite grasp Beaver's meaning.

'You aren't allowed in 'ere,' he said, pointing the revolting stem of his pipe at Beaver. 'If you want the train you'll have to go down to the station.'

'I do not want any blasted train. I want you to open the bridge.'

'Ah, I can't do that, you see. Not without I get the all clear.'

'But we've been waiting a quarter of an hour.'

'So 'ave I, so 'ave I. I reckon 'e be a bit late.'

Beaver resorted to hurt dignity. 'Do I understand that we are expected to swan about in front of this bridge until this train arrives? How do I know it's not been cancelled or something?'

The signalman was quite patient, rather as if humouring a lunatic.

'Now, you look 'ere. If I opens that there bridge and that train comes along 'e's liable to fall in the river, isn't 'e now? You wouldn't like that, would you? I'm sure you'd feel very much upset if you saw that train come tumbling down into twenty foot o' water. Think of them passengers.'

Beaver sighed. 'I am not asking you to commit man-slaughter. Put one signal at danger to stop the train. Then open the bridge. Then shut the bridge. Then put the signal at green. It's easy.'

The signalman digested this for a moment and then shook his head.

'Ah, you see it isn't as easy as all that. Not by a long chalk.'

Beaver was slowly turning purple and about to make a rude retort when a bell tinkled.

'You're in luck,' said the signalman. ' 'E's coming.'

The train crossed the bridge as we slithered down the embankment. The bridge opened as we ploughed across the field. Arthur sailed triumphantly through. The bridge shut just as we jumped aboard and cast off.

For one moment I thought Beaver would have a stroke. Instead he contented himself with going straight below and compiling an immediate letter to British Railways beginning *Dear Filth . . .*

We didn't see him again until Harry sailed us through ten minutes later and we tied up at the Reedham village staithe.

Gentle Waterways, New Thrills

'First, the waters are smooth, and the tides and currents gentle. The reed-cushioned banks are never far away, and the water is mostly shallow—though deep enough for your boat. It is a safely-adventurous holiday, with new thrills which old hands regularly enjoy.'

Extract from a Broads holiday boat catalogue

Eight

THE encounter with the signalman had wounded Beaver deeply. As soon as we had tied up he strode ashore, posted his letter of complaint to British Railways, and then marched straight into the Nelson Inn where Harry, Sheila and I found him drinking beer with primeval noises, and muttering to himself.

The Nelson used to be a fine old pub. At least it may not have been everybody's idea of a pub but it was mine. It had a smoke-stained old ceiling, a picture of the ships of the British Navy in 1899 (and an incredible lot they were too) and a real atmosphere. It was here that one year the girls shaved off Dennis's beard in the snug and later we condemned him to death and hauled him up the mast by fixing a jib halyard in his belt.

Now progress has overtaken the Nelson, like many other fine old places. The brewers have 'improved' it with plastic tables and rebuilding, and of course they've thrown the 'Ships of the British Navy' in the dustbin. I've no doubt some people think it's a better place, but I don't. I often wonder why brewers waste so much money imposing an alien character on an old place when they could spend the money better by improving the quality of the beer. There used to be many fine old pubs on the Broads, and some are losing their character as the brewers turn them into imitations of 1930 Great West Road gin-palaces. A lot have actually installed juke-boxes, the thunderous beat of which rings monotonously out over the water, ruining everyone's peace. Well, let the publicans and brewers note that I, for one, won't buy beer in any public house with a juke-box playing. I'd as soon drink in an aircraft-engine test shed.

However, they still sell beer at the Nelson, which is the main thing I suppose, and the crew of *Quiet Dawn* soon joined us, with the exception of Joan, who was scouring Reedham for breadcrumbs for Duchess potatoes. When Sheila heard this she left and joined her for another branch meeting of the Women's Consolidated Trade Union. It's odd that women don't realize how few and precious are the drinking hours allowed to us. I can think of nothing more frustrating than waiting for women to join you in a pub. They tidy their hair, change their skirts, go back for their cigarettes and then change their whole outfit because the other girls are wearing slacks. Now I don't wait for women to come to the pub. I did one year when I was skipper and we found ourselves arriving just as the landlord called last orders.

And after all that women inevitably bleat at closing time, 'Oh, are they shutting already?'

Beaver was not exactly sociable. He was further upset by a tactless remark of Arthur, who said: 'I envy yew going in that there signal box. Do you think the signalman would show me round if I flashed my Enfield Model Railway Club badge?' He sat on a stool at the end of the bar, breathing heavily, chewing cigarettes and pouring gin into his beer. Arthur held forth at great length about the state of the railways round there and every time a train hooted leaped to the door. But it was pleasant enough, especially when the girls joined us in about half an hour, although I thought Joan showed signs of strain again when Dennis cross-examined her about the shrimp sauce.

At closing time Beaver broke a long silence by remarking suddenly: 'No lunch. I'm going to try to make Norwich.'

We glanced at one another. The combination of seven pints of bitter and several gins, together with Beaver's hurt pride, was likely to prove dangerous. Arthur shrugged and said:

'I reckon we'll have our shrimp sauce and Duchess potatoes first.'

After a brief mutiny by the crew of *Merryweather II* it was agreed to allow five minutes for a cold collation. We had scarcely sat down before Beaver arose and started to hoist sail by himself, muttering and chuntering away. He did not make a very good job of it because halfway through the proceedings the gaff crashed to the deck, narrowly missing Harry's head. Finally he hoisted the sails in an appalling mess, vanished into the cabin and came back with a bottle of gin, helping himself liberally to the contents. Eventually he just sat glassy-eyed in the stern, grunting.

Beaver was tight.

Arthur and Dennis were having their lemon-meringue pie as we sailed (Dennis was telling Joan it was a little overdone). We didn't make a very good start because Beaver steered us straight into the reeds on the other side of the river, but finally we lurched off in an unsteady fashion in the general direction of Norwich. Beaver's behaviour became more and more erratic, and the gin bottle emptier and emptier. At Reedham chain-ferry he cut across the bows of the ferry which stopped just before its chains would have carted us clean out of the water, and a mile further on he deliberately sailed into a herd of swans (or is it a pride of swans?). Beaver hates swans, having been attacked by one as a child, and this gave him the idea of catching one, so for some time we sailed slowly back and forth while I held out an ingenious trap in the shape of a piece of bread on the end of a fork, and Harry held a noose of string on the end of a stick.

The idea was that the swan would swim up to take the bread, then I would carefully withdraw the bait so that the swan had no choice but to put its head in the noose. We never planned what to do with the swan when caught (they belong to the Queen, don't they?), but as we did not catch any the problem did not arise. I was rather pleased when the swans went away to attack a small boy in a rowing-boat, because one of the first things I ever learned is that a swan can break a man's arm with its wing, since when I have imagined that they do nothing else.

Then we heard the steady thud-thudding of a steamer behind us. The Yare is a busy commercial route and quite large ocean-going ships use it, sailing direct to Norwich from the Continent via Yarmouth. They have no room to manœuvre in the narrow river and all a yacht can do is to get out of the way. This is not always easy, because while the steamers normally stick to the centre of the river they reserve the right to take the outside of a bend where the water is deeper or to go near either bank if it suits them. In other words, they are right whatever happens.

When we first saw the ship it was about three hundred yards away, appearing to sail along the flat fields, thanks to a curve in the river.

'Beaver,' said Harry. 'There's a steamer behind.'

Beaver glowered at it with bloodshot eyes and took another swig of gin.

'Just too bad, isn't it?' he replied.

We sailed on, ghosting down the centre of the river with a feeble wind on the beam, and no sound but the steamer's engines and Beaver's breathing. The sugar-beet factory at Cantley was just ahead. That part of the river is protected by trees on one bank which cut down the wind, so we had little way, and the ship was catching up quickly. When it was about a hundred yards away it appeared to fill the whole river.

I coughed.

'Beaver,' I said, 'it's rather close. We could run into the bank nicely until it's past.'

Beaver looked at it again. 'It's a dirty foreign tramp,' he replied with a vile drunken belch. 'I don't give way to foreign vessels.' (I must add that Beaver has all his savings in Cunard Steamship shares.)

Harry showed signs of nervousness He had a wife and children to think of. We could read the steamer's name quite plainly. It was French. We reached a bend and the wind now came from ahead. Beaver started to tack without a glance behind him.

When he made the first tack we all thought he had come to his senses and was clearing the steamer's path. The atmosphere lightened immediately. Harry started to light a cigarette, Sheila smiled and waved at the ship and Beaver took another drink of gin. But when we neared the bank he put the helm down and came about across the river. Next moment we were heading for a point three feet in front of the steamer's bows.

A wall of steel towered over us. Two startled French faces capped by berets peered over the ship's rail. Beaver stared ahead unseeing, his eyes glazed.

'Not giving way to power vessel,' he said thickly. 'British yacht never gives way to damn' foreign tramp. Harry, tell the Frog to get out of my way.'

Beaver gibbered at it . . .

I believe that the *Manual of Seamanship* lays down that when a ship's master goes insane the officers may agree to relieve him of his command. The proper procedure is to say politely, 'Will you retire to your cabin, sir?'

Unfortunately there was no time for such niceties. Harry seized the helm and tore it from Beaver's grasp. Beaver promptly snatched it back and they sawed it to and fro for a moment, until the gin bottle fell on to the deck and Beaver relinquished the tiller to make a grab at it.

The steamer missed us by what seemed a foot but may have been four or five. Beaver gibbered at it in an ecstasy of rage and finally flung the gin bottle at the stern. Harry steered the boat straight into the bank and we all just lay there with every emotion drained from us. Sheila was down below, praying, I believe. From over the water came a voice.

'Boyur,' it called, 'what are yew doing in them reeds?'

I never thought I should be glad to hear Arthur's voice. Normally, given a choice between listening to Arthur and standing next to a pneumatic drill, I would choose the drill every time. But on this occasion it sounded like the trumpets of Paradise, a call so clear and sweet that it pierced my very soul. I sat up and stared round like someone waking from deep sleep. *Quiet Dawn* was gently gliding over the river towards us. Joan peered excitedly over the side of the cockpit, holding a half-peeled potato.

'Did you see that big steamer?' she said. 'Wasn't it fun?'

'Pull into the bank,' I told Arthur weakly, ignoring Joan's well-chosen remark. 'We've had a spot of bother.'

Suddenly everyone was talking. The silence broke up into a torrent of conversation, as when a schoolmaster leaves the classroom. Everybody babbled at the tops of their voices, saying what heroes they were and how they had never been so scared in all their lives, and the only silent person was old Beaver who sat glaring malevolently at the reeds. Then he stood up, swaying, and said: 'I don't feel well. Wanna lie down. Everything's going round and round. *Troppo multo* gin.'

He crawled into the cabin with a last slurred appeal, 'Wake me before Norwich.' He was asleep within ten seconds.

Arthur shook his head sagely when he heard the story,

which lost nothing in the telling, and he recalled a time when he and Beaver had a similar disagreement with an aircraft-carrier off Portsmouth.

'You'd have thought a naval vessel would have had the courtesy to give way,' he said, 'but she just kept on as if she owned the place. Mind you, I think Beaver was a little quixotic this time. He was morally right but practically wrong if you ask me.'

'He was drunk,' said Sheila acidly.

An unearthly moan from the cabin added point to her words.

We had a cup of tea and discussed what to do next. Norwich seemed a long way away and the trip would mean a lot of quanting because of heavily wooded banks. Arthur wanted to stop at Brundall so that he could visit the railway station there, which he said was the scene of an historic collision many years ago, but we overruled him and decided on Bramerton Woodsend, a quiet, pretty spot a mile or two beyond Brundall.

It was heavy going. The tide turned against us and we swung the quant pole until our arms ached. It was well after tea-time when we reached Bramerton and we were all so hot and tired that we stripped off for a swim, with the exception of Sheila, and Beaver, who remained unconscious.

That was a delightful swim. I don't think I have ever had a better. We plunged and gambolled around as merry as crickets. Sheila sat in the boat and threw bread to us and we all pretended to be ducks. Then Arthur did his imitation of a submarine, Harry tried to life-save Joan (and nearly drowned her) and Dennis chased a swan.

When the fun was at its height a small child rowed towards us inexpertly and sat staring.

'Hullo, sonny,' I said jovially, catching hold of his gunwale for a rest. 'Aren't you coming in for a swim?'

He didn't reply at once, but continued to brood. He then delivered himself of the following dictum: 'I suppose people have got to go to the lavatory, haven't they?'

I didn't like this.

'Yes,' he went on. 'My dad won't let me swim in the river here. It's the sewage, he says.'

The sun went in. Somehow the water didn't seem so nice.

Arthur was just diving under the surface and spouting like a whale. I shuddered.

The relentless child went on:

'It comes down on the ebb tide from the dyke, my dad says. My dad says he wouldn't swim in this part of the river for all the beer in Norwich, my dad says.'

'Where's the sewer?'

The boy pointed to a bend in the river. 'Just round the corner. They open the gates when the tide's ebbing, *like what it is now.*'

I did not swim madly to the bank. I kept my head, paddling very carefully in a bizarre fashion, holding my body perfectly upright with my face as far away from contact with the water as possible. As I dare not open my mouth, I didn't warn the others until I reached the bank. The effect was rather interesting, like the result of ringing the Lutine Bell at Lloyd's.

Joan went berserk, poor girl, and shrieked, 'Oh no, it's all your fault, Dennis,' and swam to the bank as if pursued by a jet-propelled piece of effluent. Dennis went pale and tense and by some remarkable feat of muscular control actually launched himself out of the water from the waist upwards and moved vertically to the bank. Arthur feigned indifference and hooted with bucolic laughter, but I noticed he got to the bank first.

We were only just in time. The sewage dyke announced its presence in no uncertain fashion five minutes later.

Looking on the chart we found the following legends marked near our mooring:

Sewage Works (Norwich Corporation)
Sewage Farm
Sewage Wharf
Sewage Dyke
Sewage Outlet
Old Sewer.

For good measure the bank was marked as lined with old wrecks and there was an inscription: 'Palaeolithic Implements found A.D. 1926.' What a place to put Palaeolithic implements.

But, as Arthur said, it was just as well we hadn't looked at the chart or it would have spoiled a lovely swim.

Nine

BEAVER remained deeply unconscious until we returned to the boats at closing time. Sheila had shaken him earlier and asked if he wanted any supper, but had been rewarded with a low growl of such animal intensity that she didn't ask him again.

Then, while we were having coffee over on *Quiet Dawn*, the boat rocked violently, the cabin door opened and Beaver stood framed in the aperture, looking at the point of death.

'Is it a fact that we were nearly run down this afternoon?' he croaked. 'For heaven's sake tell me if it actually happened.'

We assured him that it had happened.

'Oh, goodness me,' was his astonishing reply (the only time I think I have ever heard Beaver use the phrase). 'Oh dear, oh dear. I must have been boozed. I haven't been like that since the night the war finished in Cairo.'

We all felt quite warm to Beaver after that and assured him that the danger was much exaggerated and we were sure that even if the ship had hit us we were all good swimmers and would have survived.

Beaver's remark about V.E. Night in Cairo started a spate of reminiscence. We all knew one another's stories, of course, and waited politely for each one to finish before dashing in with our own. The formula on these occasions is to say as the laughter for the previous story dies down, 'I don't know whether I ever told you about the time I was stationed in North Wales . . .' and everyone else, who has heard the story at least twenty times before, politely mutters, 'No, no,' and then the speaker launches into a tissue of lies based on some long-forgotten original incident.

Hearing these stories every year, it was interesting to see

how they grew. Arthur, for instance, used to tell a perfectly good yarn about the time a native tailor sewed a Middlesex Regiment flash on one shoulder of his uniform and a Royal Armoured Corps flash on the other. He didn't notice this, but a military policeman did, and stopped him on suspicion of being a German spy (only a military policeman could have thought that). Just then an officer in his unit came by and vouched for him and all was put right, except that Arthur got seven days for being improperly dressed.

This story had now reached a version in which Arthur was tied to a post facing a firing squad.

'The officer gave the command, "Ready . . . aim . . ." ' said Arthur in a hushed silence. 'I could see the rifle barrels pointing at me—I refused to be blindfolded, you see. It's an interesting thing, but they weren't all pointing at my heart, they were pointing all over me. That's orders, you see, they all aim at a different vital point. One bloke aims at your left eye, another aims at your thigh artery, another chap aims at the forehead and perhaps three or four aim at the heart. I must admit I was a bit scared. The officer was just about to say "Fire!" when a motor-cyclist dashed up, drove in front of the firing squad and shouted: "Don't fire. He's innocent!" They'd found my pay-book which I'd lost in the canteen. Another minute and I'd have been a gonner.'

It's a tribute to Arthur's powers of story-telling that this preposterous tale still impressed us.

But Dennis had a good story which never failed, and it was true. He recalled becoming extremely drunk at a wedding in 1950 and driving his car through the front garden fence. When his mother protested he said, 'I'm sorry, I haven't been like this since I was in Rome in 1945.'

'There you are,' said his mother triumphantly, 'it's becoming a habit with you.'

After the day's events we went to bed tired but happy, apart from a slight whiff of sewage from the river.

It was about 2 a.m. when I was awakened by a dreadful groaning. I switched on the cabin light and saw Beaver tossing and turning from side to side. I asked him what was the matter and he replied, 'Piles,' in a hollow voice.

Harry and Sheila were awake now and Sheila asked solicitously if there was anything that could be done. At first Beaver suggested a bullet through his brain but then he recalled having some suppositories in his suitcase.

Sheila, who was in the forepeak, searched the suitcase and couldn't find any trace of the healing suppositories, but confessed perhaps that was because she didn't know what they looked like. Harry said he knew, so he searched the case, and he drew a blank as well. By this time I was contemptuous of their failure, so I had a look. True, I didn't know what a suppository looked like, in fact I didn't even know what it was, but I was sure if there was anything medical in that case I'd find it. Well, I turned it inside out and uncovered a fearful mess of stuff inside: dirty socks, old underwear, a compass, a pocket chess set and a flask of brandy, but nothing that could have been described as a suppository.

Of course I was looking for something like those strange straps and pads that hang in shabby surgical shops up the Charing Cross Road. I asked Beaver what they really looked like and he refused to discuss them or the method of treatment while Sheila was present. He made an effort to look for them himself, but the discomfort of crawling into the forepeak was too much and he gave up.

Sleep was impossible while Beaver kept complaining, so Harry got out the medicinal stores and poured him out half a tumbler of brandy, into which he crushed six aspirins, and then added some hot water.

Beaver's first reaction to this was to become talkative, and recall past occasions on which this illness, a family curse equal to that upon the ancient Scottish clans, had laid him low. But by the time he had drunk the whole glass his voice slurred and in the middle of some rambling reminiscence he fell asleep.

We all slept.

In the morning Beaver was no better and stayed in his bunk. A council of war was held and we decided to carry on with the schedule in the hope that he would recover. Norwich was now out of the question, so the day's target was set as Beccles, a tough run but well worth it, for the Waveney, on which Beccles lies, is one of the pleasantest rivers on the Broads.

The day was sunny, warm and calm, and I hummed to myself while cleaning my teeth. Joan was cooking omelettes on the next boat and I heard Dennis reject his with the comment, 'No, thanks, my shoes don't want soling and heeling today.' I wondered how long Joan would stand for it.

There was hardly a breath of wind as both boats quanted together back down the river, the sails flapping idly. Every so often a faint puff came, invariably from a different direction each time, and after a time we ignored these false alarms and slogged away in shifts of twenty minutes each.

Beaver recovered sufficiently to take an interest in what was going on, and having viewed the situation through a port-hole demanded that we make bigger efforts to overtake Arthur, who had crept ahead.

We stepped up the quanting rate just for the fun of it and Arthur, who can't resist a challenge, promptly accepted. Within a few minutes a demoniac struggle was going on. I've seen this sort of thing happen before, usually between Beaver and another boat. The race goes on until someone collapses or the wind springs up.

This time Dennis tried to steal a march by towing *Quiet Dawn*. As soon as we were clear of the trees he hopped ashore with a long line which Arthur always orders from the boatyard for such emergencies and trudged along the bank. This was fine until he came to an inaccessible section of the bank and had to relinquish the rope. Arthur drifted on while Dennis tried to find a way through the trees. He vanished from sight and then there was a long-drawn-out howl, like that of a wolf for her lost mate. When Dennis finally appeared it was obvious that he had fallen into a particularly nasty bog.

The wind gradually improved as the morning wore on and we reached Reedham by lunch. On the way we made a small detour up the dyke to Surlingham Broad so that we could say we had at least seen a Broad. Thanks to the various crises, it didn't look as if we were going to have time for anything more than battering up and down the rivers. We had to stop temporarily at Reedham because Dennis's cat fell overboard while chasing a butterfly, but we resisted the temptation to visit the Nelson as we had a long way to go.

After the cat was rescued Sheila had the bright idea of closeting it with Beaver, thinking it would cheer him up, rather as they tried to cheer up King David in his old age by presenting him with maidens. The idea was sound in theory, but it did not work. After two minutes there was a scuffling and a squawking below and Beaver called out that he was being clawed to death by a wild animal which had got into the cabin (he was asleep when the cat entered).

Sheila went into the cabin and found that the cat had its claws entangled in Beaver's beard, so neither of them could move but just lay staring at each other. It was such an unusual sight that we all came in to have a look, which did not please Beaver. Harry said, 'We'll just have to cut off your beard, Beaver,' which produced a roar of protest and the counter-suggestion we cut off the cat's legs.

Sheila solved things by stroking Pussy until he relaxed his claws and he was transferred back to *Quiet Dawn* by means of a rugby pass which would not have disgraced an international scrum-half.

The swing bridge gave us no trouble this time, because it opened for a cargo steamer and we crept through behind it. This time, instead of retracing our route along the Yare, we swung off along the New Cut, which like most New Cuts was built about a hundred and fifty years ago. This particular one was dug to provide a short cut for wherries travelling to Norwich from Lowestoft and Beccles, and now it serves the same purpose for pleasure craft. It used to be spanned by a charming little lifting bridge, which we nicknamed the Van Gogh Bridge. If you didn't want the bother of taking down the mast you had to tell the signalman by the railway line, and a few minutes later a porter would cycle along and open the bridge, charging a toll of two shillings. Now the bridge is replaced by a modern road bridge, doubtless much more efficient but much less fun and not so quaint.

The New Cut joins the Waveney near Haddiscoe railway swing bridge. The wind had dropped here and we drifted out of the cut helped by a desultory poke or two with the quant. The tide was running strongly upstream towards the bridge, which was open. It was lovely to be on the Waveney again and

Sheila filled the kettle for tea. Harry stopped quanting and lit a cigarette.

The signalman leaned out of his box and shouted that he was going to close the bridge.*

I put the helm over to come about and nothing happened. We had no steerage way and continued to drift slightly sideways down on to the bridge. Harry jumped up, knocking the kettle over, and seized the quant pole. As usual when you need it in a hurry, it had entangled itself in the shrouds. They are malevolent things, quant poles. When you don't need them, of course, they obtrude themselves, getting in the way on every possible occasion, but when they're wanted in a hurry they go on strike and tie themselves up in the nearest rope. In the end Harry freed the pole and plunged it into the water.

It would not touch bottom.

'Don't close the bridge,' I shouted to the signalman.

'Train's on the way,' he replied, and added as an afterthought: 'And the trains round here don't float.'

The bridge began to close. Harry threw the quant pole on the deck and began to paddle with the cabin mop. Sheila paddled with a frying-pan. I waggled the tiller. But it was too late.

As the bridge swung across I had just a moment of delirious exultation. Surely this was the sort of thing old Jem Green would have revelled in? After all, I was at the helm, the man in command.

I see the tiny ketch being pounded to pieces in full view of the little fishing village, while the villagers fire off maroons in all directions and sing 'Abide With Me' on the quayside.

I cup my hands to my mouth, the rain streaming from my oilskins.

'Lower the boat, lads. Look lively.'

'Us caaaan't, Cap'n Jem. 'Er be stuck, loike.'

I stride from the tiny bridge to the boat falls, and with one blow of my ham-sized fist free the jammed pulley, using the other hand to pull back some craven-hearted coward trying to get in the boat first.

* Since this was written the railway line has been closed and Haddiscoe Bridge is always open, thank heavens.

Old Jem Green

'There you are, lads. Jump in quick now.'

The frail boat is lowered, perilously full.

'Jump, Cap'n. Jump in before it's too late.'

'Not I, lads. There's no room. Save yourselves. I order yew.'

'God bless yew, Cap'n. Yew be a right 'un, yew be. Push off, lads.'

I raise my arm in salutation. The village choir change to 'Those In Peril on the Sea'. The boat gives a lurch. With a growl of defiance, I fling myself into the churning sea and strike for the shore, not even bothering to take off my oilskins.

A sinister clanking cut short my reverie. The bridge was closing. Jem Green faded and a pallid city-dweller took his place.

'Every man and woman for himself,' I squeaked ungrammatically. Harry pushed a reluctant Sheila over, jumped himself and I followed. We looked rather silly floundering in the water looking up at the bridge.

At this moment I realized Beaver was asleep on his bunk below.

The bridge caught the mast as it swung closed and the boat heeled to an alarming angle. There was a sharp crack and the mast fell down.

What followed is rather confused in my mind. Certainly the most noise came from the boat, where it appeared a young bull had been let loose. There were blastings and swearings and cursings as we swam towards our battered hulk to reboard it. Finally Beaver stuck his head out of the cabin door, stared at the tangled wreckage about him, and simply said, 'Upon my pile.'

He didn't even offer us a hand as Harry and I clambered aboard (Sheila had wisely swum to the bank), but continued to gaze about him, calling upon his illness every so often.

While we were making for the bank as best we could the bridge opened, Arthur sailed through without any trouble at all and started the conversation by asking if we had noticed the unusual locomotive that had just passed over. Harry said no, but he had noticed the unusual yacht that had just passed under, the one without a mast and with a bearded lunatic gibbering in the cabin doorway.

'Come to think of it, yew have lost your mast, haven't yew?' pronounced Arthur, after a long look at the wreckage. 'What are you going to do, like?'

'Mike is going to ring the boatyard,' put in Beaver firmly from the cabin, where he had retired.

'Oh no, I'm not,' I retorted. 'I'm not going to face that bloke Loudwater. You know him best. You've had this sort of accident before.'

'That's exactly why I don't want to speak to him,' said Beaver with some logic. 'Besides, you were at the helm. It's your responsibility.'

'Let Arthur do it,' I suggested. 'As it's not his boat, Loudwater can't complain.'

Arthur shrank. 'No fear, I wouldn't ring old Loudwater for all the tea in China.'

I went to find a phone.

This was not easy and when I did find a call-box the bell rang a long time without answer. That was a bad sign. It meant someone would be coming a long way to reply and would be in a bad temper. I could imagine Loudwater himself being awoken from a siesta by the riverside and painfully limping to the telephone. However, just as I was about to put down the receiver there was an answer.

'Hello,' said a soft Norfolk voice. 'Loudwater's yard.'

'Ah.' I ran out of anything to say and prevaricated. 'Is that Mr. Loudwater's yard?'

'Yes. Loudwater's yard here.'

'Er . . . is Mr. Loudwater there?'

'No.'

'Thank God—I mean how distressing. . . . You see, this is *Merryweather II* here. . . . We've had a spot of bother. . . . Ha, ha, ha, nothing much really, ha, ha, ha. . . .'

'*Merryweather II*, eh? You're the people that had that trouble at Potter, didn't you? Boat with a bearded skipper, chap as knows Mr. Loudwater?'

'Yes, that's us. We—ha, ha—well, the fact of the matter is . . . ha, ha . . . we've lost our mast.'

There was a long silence. Then the man said:

'Dear, dear, dear, dear, dear. Oh, dearie me, I don't know what Mr. Loudwater's going to say about that. I'll have to cycle up to his house and tell him, you know.'

'Do, by all means,' I said magnanimously. After all, we couldn't object to Loudwater knowing we had wrecked his boat. 'But what are you going to do about it?'

The man wasn't sure. We were to quant to St. Olave's Bridge and they'd try to send a lorry round with a new mast. Perhaps tomorrow morning, perhaps never. It depended on how Mr. Loudwater felt.

'By the way,' he added, 'Mr. Loudwater's very upset about that business at Potter. You know that woman who had hysterics hasn't left her bunk yet? Just lies there moaning and groaning. You've let us in for something you have and no mistake.'

I was rather pleased when that conversation finished.

As might have been expected, there was no praise for my heroic deed when I returned to the boats. Beaver said I should have insisted on speaking to Loudwater personally and given him a piece of my mind about his short quant poles which wouldn't touch bottom in a crisis and his rotten masts which fell down at a touch. Dennis said I should have demanded a new mast within the hour or else threatened to stop our cheque.

Poor old *Merryweather* was an awful mess. We tidied her up as best we could and quanted the mile or so to St. Olave's, downstream, where we laid the broken mast on the bank and prepared everything as far as possible to make the repair easier.

While doing this we made an interesting discovery. The bowsprit was undamaged.

This seemed impossible, because the bowsprit helps to support the mast by means of the forestay, and if the mast snaps then the forestay must snap the bowsprit. Further investigation was made and an alarming fact came to light.

Someone had not made the forestay fast after we had re-erected the mast for the New Cut Bridge.

It's extraordinary, but, although it was only an hour or two since we had taken down the mast and put it up again, no one could remember whose job it had been to make the forestay fast. Everyone could remember that it wasn't *him*, but that was as far as we got. By mutual consent we dropped the topic, although we knew that for the rest of our lives we should be whispering to each other that it really was so-and-so who didn't make fast the forestay the day we lost the mast.

Of course, it's all exaggerated . . .

'. . . the quant would not hold bottom so far out and we watched our boat drift broadside on into a lump of darkness pierced only by the glimmering hole of the low side arch. Across that we stuck fast, our bowsprit shaking like a reed with the strain. An attempt to make her lie more comfortably, or haply to get her stern through the arch by hauling ashore on a line from her head, resulted in such an ominous crashing of planks in the dark, as made us prefer to sit all night supperless, watching for dawn and the ebb tide.

We floated off in the cold grey morning, and a gale sprang up against us that rendered the first reach unsailable. . . . Five or six times we hopelessly set ourselves to quant up that reach without breakfast and as often we were drifted down; at a certain point we either had to go ashore or the quant lost bottom.'

Extract from an article 'A Cruise on the Norfolk Broads' by R. A. M. Stevenson, M.A., in *Outdoor Games and Recreations*, published by The Religious Tract Society in 1892. The author is describing an attempt to shoot Somerleyton Swing Bridge in the dark.

Ten

THAT night the cat died.

It must have been heart failure after the day's events. Arthur found he had passed away as he made his usual stroll round the deck at dawn. Pussy was buried before breakfast after a pathetic ceremony in which the little cadaver was gently lowered in a shallow grave in some nearby marshes. A wreath made of reeds was laid on top and the whole surmounted by a picture postcard of Potter Heigham bearing the words POOR PUSSY.

I like to think someone would do as much for me some time.

Not unnaturally, this event cast a gloom over the proceedings (as the local newspaper said when a mourner fell into the grave and broke his leg). We were a sorry crowd as we sat drinking our third cup of coffee and waiting for Loudwater's lorry. However, in the middle of our misery Beaver emerged from the cabin whooping with joy and clutching a small packet.

'I've found them!' he cried. 'I've found them!'

'Found what?' asked Harry.

'My suppositories. They were tucked in the end of my shoe. You don't know what this means to me.'

It must have been a long time since anyone at St. Olave's had bawled the word 'suppository' at the top of his voice and several startled faces were turned in our direction, especially as Beaver was so overjoyed that he danced round all the moored boats, waving his little packet triumphantly and shouting the good news to all and sundry. I'm sure one or two people thought he had won the Pools. Anyway, they congratulated him and he shook hands and showed them his little packet and seemed surprised when their faces dropped and they backed away in alarm.

Beaver now vanished for five minutes.

He returned wreathed in smiles and exuding bonhomie all round. Those little things must be wonderful.

Loudwater's lorry arrived at nine-thirty with a brand-new mast sticking out fore and aft. I retired to a safe distance in case Loudwater himself was there and wanted to cross-examine the helmsman, but he wasn't, although one of the men said he had taken to his bed after hearing of the accident.

It took about two hours to step a new mast and a very fine job they made of it. Norfolk boatyard craftsmen are superb, and take a great pride in their work, although they sometimes adopt a cynical air. I remember one year when Beaver had to have an emergency repair to a great gash ripped in his bow and after completing a beautifully polished piece of work the yardman merely commented, 'A rough old job, but it'll last till the end of the season.'

No sooner was everything ready than Beaver, now his old self, demanded an instant start for Beccles. None of us was very keen because it would mean a terribly long journey the next day, which was the last full day of the trip. But Beaver produced a load of optimistic figures about how easy it would be with the tide if we got up at dawn and we gave in. Besides, we really like Beccles. It's our favourite spot.

We sailed without any startling incident for about an hour in a fair breeze, but about two o'clock signs of disturbance were noticed on board *Quiet Dawn*. Voices were raised in the well, Joan's being prominent among them. Beaver sailed as close as possible so that we could spy on them and we heard Joan saying: 'No, I won't cook you any lunch. I spend all my time kneeling on this wretched floor with Dennis's stinking feet treading all over me while you two have all the fun. You can cook the lunch and I'll sail the boat.'

Dennis and Arthur regarded her rather as the beadle must have regarded Oliver Twist when he asked for more.

'Sail the boat?' exclaimed Dennis. 'You must be joking, girl. Now get on and put that spaghetti on to boil. We're hungry.'

'Ah,' added Arthur. 'I haven't eaten for two hours.'

'No,' said Joan firmly. 'You put on your own rotten spaghetti and I hope it chokes you.'

Dennis tried wheedling. 'But, Joan,' he said, 'you don't know how to sail the boat.'

'Then you teach me. And I must say that from what I've seen of Mike I could sail as well as him' (that was most unfair).

The argument went on for about ten minutes, during which their sailing suffered and we drew ahead. However, we were delayed by a gentleman in what appeared to be a floating saloon bar who drove us into the reeds and *Quiet Dawn* hove into view round the bend. At first I thought she was on fire. A dense cloud of white smoke covered the well and a voice was calling out oaths and curses. I then realized that the smoke was steam and it was coming from a pot of boiling water in the cooking locker. Arthur was on the deck tending the pot by abusing it, its contents and its mother in a loud voice. He had apparently burnt himself and had one hand stuck in his jacket like Napoleon.

Joan was steering.

The wind was on the beam so she couldn't really go wrong, and Dennis was holding the sheets and directing her, every so often putting his hand over his eyes as she headed for the bank or another boat.

Beaver slowed our progress so that we could enjoy the scene. I'm glad he did so, for I saw a sight that will live long in the memory, even longer than my recollection of the vicar blowing up his church hall while working the effects for an amateur performance of *Journey's End*. As *Quiet Dawn* rounded the bend and the wind came from astern, Joan allowed her to gybe and the boom clouted Arthur across the cockpit as he was about to drain the water from the spaghetti.

The boiling water must have gone over Dennis's feet because he rose like a helicopter and hopped about the well. Arthur raised an anguished hand smothered in hot spaghetti and began wringing his hands to get rid of the stuff (a good deal of it flew across Joan's face, giving her an interesting appearance).

Quiet Dawn was approaching a boat moored by the bank in which four Sea Scouts were enjoying a meal. Joan put the helm over to clear them and put it the wrong way. As often happens with a novice, when she found she was pushing instead of

pulling she merely pushed all the harder. *Quiet Dawn* turned
neatly and headed for the Sea Scouts' boat with naval accuracy.
  'Joan,' shouted Harry. 'Pull it the other way.'

Joan was steering

Joan turned and gave him a ghastly, hysterical smile, before pushing the helm even further. Dennis and Arthur were still wrapped up in their injuries and didn't even notice what was happening.

It was an odd sort of collision. *Quiet Dawn*'s bowsprit went neatly through a port-hole on the Scouts' boat, almost as if it had been aimed there. There was a crunch, a tinkle, a chorus of surprised voices, and there she was swinging gently with her bowsprit in the Scouts' cabin.

At least the collision shut up Dennis and Arthur for a moment. Joan sat in the stern staring at her handiwork and then burst into tears.

The Scouts were very decent about it (one suspects they had done the same thing themselves in the past). They also insisted on applying first-aid to Dennis, Arthur and Joan, as well as one of their own crew who had been sleeping on a bunk when *Quiet Dawn*'s bowsprit entered the cabin like a swordfish coming aboard.

They were very keen and rather overdid the first-aid. By the time they had finished Dennis looked like one of those cartoons of people with gout and Arthur had his left arm tied to his right leg by six feet of bandages. He complained bitterly about this and they took it all off and replaced it so that his right arm was tied to his left leg, and he lost his temper and tore all the bandages away. Joan was treated as a serious case of shock and hysteria and the first Scout to approach her clouted her violently on the face and poured a bowl of water over her.

As she was not hysterical, she merely burst into even louder sobs, crying: 'Why do you let them attack me like this? Won't anyone stop them?'

However, in the end it was all sorted out and we parted on good terms. After that Arthur and Dennis sailed *Quiet Dawn* into Beccles.

We reached Beccles about seven. It had been a hard, thirsty day, with a fair amount of quanting on the final stretch, and as soon as sail was down and stowed on both boats all the men started to march off for a quick one before supper.

Sheila and Joan had been muttering together by the staithe

and Sheila stopped us by calling out, 'Hey, where do you lot think you're going?'

'To the boozer,' Harry replied patiently, as if explaining something to a dense child.

'You're not,' said Sheila. 'You're cooking the supper. Joan and I are going to the boozer.'

'I believe the women are revolting,' said Harry.

'I know they are, but they can't help it,' said Dennis smartly. This did not help matters. There was a tightening of female lips and a tossing of curly heads.

'Don't be silly,' was Beaver's contribution. He found conversation with women difficult and the situation was beyond him.

'This is mutiny,' said Arthur. 'Mutiny is an ugly word.'

'Joan and I are merely being sensible for the first time,' said Sheila firmly. 'Are you men going to cook supper or not?'

'But I cooked the lunch,' said Dennis in a pained voice.

The girls' reply was to roar with laughter.

Surprisingly it was Beaver who let us down.

'All right,' he told the girls. 'We'll cook supper. And we'll show you just how it should be done. Only you've got to go and have a drink and pay for it yourselves. Is that fair?'

The girls agreed it was, and off they went with much giggling.

To make the preparation easier it was decided to have a joint meal between the boats. There was a certain amount of cooking experience among us, gained painfully in bed-sitters in Birmingham and Earls Court, and we were by no means helpless. With great cunning it was decided to have a real tinned feast, starting with tinned soup, followed by tinned stew with tinned peas and carrots, and rounded off with tinned fruit and cream. We could not go wrong and as an extra treat Arthur undertook to make some dehydrated mashed potato.

There seemed no point in putting on the stew until the girls were in sight, as it would be hot enough by the time the soup course was over, so we broached the medicinal stores and smoked and told jokes and swapped yarns. Then as we saw the girls coming across the grass to the staithe we all bustled to our respective jobs.

Harry was chief cook; my job was opening cans. I'm a great one for can-opening, I've had so much practice in my life. I just flew at every can in sight and opened it wildly, while Harry poured the contents into the saucepan, giving it a professional stir every so often.

First there were three tins of stew and then the tins of vegetables and then the fruit and cream. I knelt on the deck opening away and passing them up like a conveyor belt. At last I finished the final can and as I did so Harry gave a little gasp. He was peering into the saucepan with an odd expression.

'Mike,' he said in a strained voice. 'I've poured the pine-apples and mandarins into the stew.'

We dined off soup, mashed potatoes and cheese.

When the girls complained I pointed out that during the war I had eaten an exactly similar meal which the orderly officer had described as 'a nutritious and satisfying dinner'.

Afterwards we adjourned to the Cambridge public house, as we do every year we visit Beccles. Old Harry, the landlord, always lets us use the back room with the harmonium on which we play dismal dirges and where we can sing without distressing the other customers too much. Harry told us of a crew he'd just seen painfully tacking to and fro across the river with the wind *behind* them.

'What are you doing, tacking with the wind behind you?' shouted Harry.

'It's all right,' came the reply. 'We know this stretch well. *We had to tack up it last year.*'

In some mysterious way, via the Broads grapevine, Harry had heard of our unpleasantness at Potter Heigham, and about our mast. Another man in the bar said Loudwater was breathing fire and slaughter but we comforted ourselves that perhaps he was exaggerating.

The evening ended with Arthur playing 'Abide with Me' on the harmonium (an elderly gentleman in the public bar was observed to cry during this) and we weaved a rather unsteady way back to the boats. We had stopped in the square to render the sentry's song from *Iolanthe* when a window was flung up violently after the first verse and I cringed in anticipation.

'That was very nice,' a man called out. 'Give us another.' I *do* like Beccles.

Back at the boats medicinal stores were broached and we continued singing in *Quiet Dawn*. It was one o'clock before we went to bed, which would give us four hours' sleep before a five o'clock start in the morning for our last complete day.

I was having a final cigarette in the well when a voice called out 'Fire!' and before I knew what was happening someone directed a hosepipe at me from the bank. Having thoroughly soaked the whole boat they retreated with a cry of 'Boyur'.

All hands were immediately summoned to arms and half an hour later we crept along the bank to Arthur's boat with the intention of casting it adrift. But as Beaver, Harry and myself were creeping along the bank on all fours a policeman cycled up, shone his torch at us and asked what we were doing.

A question like that is rather embarrassing. I suppose one could reply, 'I am crawling along the bank on all fours,' or you could say, 'It's all right, officer, I always walk like this.' But the trouble is that any Englishman confronted by the law is immediately struck into incoherence. One gathers that other nationalities are not. Russians are alleged to say: 'It is true. I see myself as a reactionary Trotskyite capitalist revanchist. I have allowed myself to be led astray by broadcasts from the filthy fascist imperialist British Broadcasting Corporation. I hope that after a long course of corrective training at a People's Volunteer Labour Camp in Siberia I shall be allowed once more to take my place in the forward march towards complete Socialism.'

Americans, if one can believe the films, make statements to the police like: 'O.K., Lootenant, so I shot Kerrigan. You wanna know why? 'Cos he was a lousy bum. He took my goil. So I ventilated him. And now put the bracelets on me and take me down the Precinct.'

But Englishmen, again if one can believe what policemen say in court, show all the national characteristics of reticence. The dialogue is reported by the police witness as follows: 'I said to him, "I have reason to believe you were skulking outside Barclay's Bank just now, with a housebreaking implement, viz. a jemmy, in your possession." He replied, "Yes."

I told him he would be arrested. He said: "You've got me bang to rights, guv'nor. I shall get six months for this." '

Good heavens, I was once myself in court for a parking offence, and the policeman made me sound like an old lag from Parkhurst. He told the magistrates:

'I told him he was forbidden to park there, and he replied: "Yes, that is right, officer. It's a fair cop. I shall get a month in stir for this. I expect I was in drink at the time. Once the bluebottles put the mark on you you don't have a chance." '

In fact I'm sure I said 'Oh, all right, if you say parking is forbidden then I suppose it is.' That's *my* story.

However, to return to the bank. Beaver solved matters by placing his beard against the constable's ear and explaining in a stage whisper that we were playing a merry jape upon some friends in another boat. The constable couldn't hear and replied, 'What did you say?' very loudly until they were almost shouting at each other. When he grasped the idea the policeman immediately entered into the spirit of things and himself began to whisper and crawl about like something out of a silent film.

When we reached *Quiet Dawn* Harry untied her and Beaver and I gave the boat a terrific push across the dyke. We were all laughing like mad, including the policeman, when from out of the darkness a jet of water appeared and hit the policeman in the face. He stopped laughing very quickly.

It was, of course, Arthur lying in ambush by the public water-tap. He mistook the policeman for Beaver in the dark and kept hosing him up and down and roaring with laughter and insulting him, and then doubling up with laughter again. Eventually the policeman got near enough to Arthur to be recognized and the water dribbled away from the end of the hose. A ghastly silence rent the air.

It took the rest of the brandy and two cups of hot coffee to pacify the policeman. I think the brandy did the trick. He was almost friendly by the time he'd finished it sitting in the cabin dripping water all over the place. There aren't many places like Beccles, more's the pity.

At three o'clock we retired to sleep.

SOME PEARLS FROM THE MUDBANKS

Small drops of water falling on the face are usually a sign of rain.

Once a packet of detergent spills into the bilge you may as well give up the trip unless you like sleeping in a cloud of foam.

If the boat smells pump out the bilge.

If it continues to smell throw out whoever it is.

Watch the seagulls—if they are walking instead of floating it is time to come about.

Beware of the man who says: 'This boat is unsinkable. I defy you to capsize her. Go on, have a try.'

Always carry a supply of visiting cards, bearing your name and address, to throw to boats which you have struck, scraped or damaged. This saves a lot of tiresome shouting.

Better still, carry a supply of someone else's visiting cards for the same purpose.

Don't let your boat's name be too easily discernible.

If there is a foul tide and no wind, and darkness falls before you can make port, *don't worry*. I'm afraid I can't think of anything that will help you, but it is absolutely essential not to worry.

Keep smiling.

Always carry a false beard unless you are insured up to the hilt.

Never sew cork into the seat of your trousers unless you are prepared to stand for the whole voyage.

It is no use telling the truth. Yachtsmen don't know what it means.

An elderly yachtsman is one who reefs too soon.

Eleven

WE AROSE at five o'clock. It was dull and overcast. There was no wind. Everyone had a hangover and felt tired after two hours' sleep. Then after quanting out of the dyke we discovered that the tide was still against us. Beaver had got us up for nothing.

The whole company turned irritably on Beaver, who gave some feeble explanation about contrary winds delaying the tide. Quanting against the tide is a mug's game and we all felt thoroughly exhausted when the wind started to rise about nine o'clock.

At St. Olave's we moored to take down the mast before going under the bridge and Arthur was dismayed to see a policeman approaching him.

After examining the boat in silence the policeman said, 'Are you the hirer of *Quiet Dawn* here?'

'I have no statement to make about last night,' said Arthur firmly. 'The officer assured me he would say nothing more and I took his word. In any case it was all a ghastly mistake.' He added with a flash of inspiration: 'I was nearly wounded at Dunkirk, you know.'

The policeman looked puzzled.

'I don't know what happened last night,' he said, 'and I don't want to know. But I do want to know if you're the boat that threw your cat overboard yesterday.'

Arthur paled. 'Well, I did have a cat like . . .'

'According to what I'm told, you tied a brick to his neck and threw him overboard.'

Arthur almost blubbered at the injustice of this.

'I never tied a brick to him. Anyway, Dennis buried him. I

wouldn't have hurt a hair of his lovely little head. He died of fright after the other boat hit the bridge. I put him in the marshes.'

'I know that. You didn't bury him very deep, did you? He floated out at high tide. As if he were accusing you, like.'

It took Arthur and Dennis half an hour to convince the policeman that they were the victims of the village gossip.

The policeman then said he was enquiring about a report concerning a boat careering around in front of steamers on the Yare. Arthur said he knew nothing about that but he had seen a cruiser behaving very mysteriously and gave the name of young Kensington's boat at Potter. I only hope Mother didn't have hysterics again.

We were glad to leave St. Olave's. Breydon looked leaden and sullen as we approached via the treacherous mouth of the Waveney. It's not easy tacking up that stretch on the ebb tide when one mistake in the narrow channel can put you aground for eight hours, or even eight days if the tide's a freak. Beaver recalled seeing a boat go aground in a gale at the top of the highest tide of the decade. It literally vanished into the reeds, which closed behind it, and when the tide went down it was almost high and dry with cows grazing around.

In fact on this occasion we passed a motor-boat which had apparently tried to cut the corner by Berney Arms and was hopelessly stuck, the occupants bleating piteously for aid.

Near the Yarmouth end of Breydon we went aground ten feet inside the marker posts (everybody who goes aground swears they were inside the posts, but this happens to be true). It was dreadfully humiliating. I was over the stern, up to my thighs in mud, vainly trying to push us off, when dear old Sinbad, the tugman, arrived and towed us off in a twinkling, free of charge, just for old times' sake. He was on his way to Berney Arms, reaping the harvest of an exceptional tide.

The water was quite warm and the mud around my thighs was warm too, so I felt like someone having an invalid bath. While Harry fixed Sinbad's towline at the bows I leaned against the stern enjoying the respite from pushing. Next moment *Merryweather II* was surging forward and I was floundering on my face. By the time I was upright and shouting she was sailing away on the port tack, Beaver and Harry handling the sheets furiously.

I really must have looked an idiot standing up to my waist in the middle of Breydon Water calling for help. It was also very uncomfortable. The tide was running so swiftly that I could feel the mud moving under my feet. To comfort myself I pulled a cigarette from the chest of my waterproof and lit it.

A motor-cruiser approached with two young men and two scantily clad girls staring in surprise at the sight of someone standing in the water smoking a cigarette.

'It's all right,' I called. 'The marker buoy has sunk and the harbour commissioners have asked me to stay here for a few hours until it's repaired. They've given me a bell in case of fog. Please keep to starboard, if you don't mind.'

Another cruiser switched course to examine me. It was driven by a bald-headed man in braces who nearly ran me down. His wife, a fat, artificial blonde, peered at me curiously.

'Aren't you cold, luv?' she said at length.

'God bless you, no, madam,' I said. 'You gets used to it. The only human buoy between here and the Nore, I be. They allus calls out old Jem Green when they be in trouble. Beware of the shoal, if you please.'

'I wouldn't like your job,' said the woman. 'Alf, do you hear what the gent says?'

Alf replied by jerking his boat into gear at full throttle and nearly running me down. I retaliated by pointing an accusing finger at him as he passed, and I like to think he was afraid of being reported.

My absence was noticed on board *Merryweather II* after they had gone a hundred yards on the tack, but for various reasons they took a long time to come up for the rescue and when they did so Beaver refused to approach nearer than twenty feet in case he ran aground again.

I stepped a pace forward to walk as close as possible to him and vanished beneath the waves. I had forgotten that the dredged channel on Breydon is twenty feet deep. By now Beaver had let the bows pay off and had to sail away again, so I was left treading water. It took him ages to bring the boat

. . . standing up to my waist in the middle of Breydon Water

round again and my cigarettes were a pulpy mess by the time Harry hauled me aboard.

The entrance to the Bure, from which we had emerged four days before, was the usual maelstrom of yachts in distress and impatient powered craft making their distress even worse. Arthur had been unable to make the turn into the Bure, as the wind was cut off by buildings and jetties, and was now painfully trying to claw his way back from the direction of Yarmouth harbour.

Merryweather nearly suffered the same fate, drifting sideways with the tide as the wind failed, but Harry rescued us with some sterling quant-pole work, and we made the coal wharf. There was an hour to wait before slack water which we occupied in getting down the mast and making tea. Arthur spent the hour sawing to and fro in the cross-currents between the Yare and Bure and calling down vengeance on them both. He had to wait until the ebb slackened before he could come in.

We quanted under the bridges at slack water and reached the yacht station at six o'clock, having been on the go for over twelve hours. The boat was due back at the yard at 10 a.m. the next day. The yard was nineteen miles away—five hours' sailing even under the very best conditions. A conference was held and we decided to try for Stracey Arms, seven miles upriver, before stopping for the night. That would at least leave a reasonable distance for the morning.

The stretch of the Bure between Yarmouth and the Stracey Arms is equally unpleasant whichever way you are travelling. True, the tide was with us, but the wind dropped as the sun went down and what little wind blew was ahead. The two boats drifted upriver sluggishly, stopping every now and then to go aground. After three hours we were at Runham Swim, two miles short of Stracey Arms. It was dark.

Hired boats are not supposed to sail after dark on the Broads, although we had done it before in emergencies. We carried on a further half-hour and then moored by a section of bank which careful sounding with the quant pole revealed to be slightly less treacherous than the rest. Even then we were careful to moor a couple of feet away, lashing the two boats fore and aft and using the mud-weights as anchors.

Usually we have a special feast on the last night, using up all the food that's left. A typical menu might contain soup, followed by eggs, bacon and tinned carrots, cold lambs' tongues in jelly, salted peanuts and a pound of cheese per person. But when the girls came to prepare they found we had no water, no bread and no tinned food with the exception of seven tins of sardines.

It was one of the most indigestible meals I have ever had in my life, consisting of sardines, boiled eggs and tomatoes, without any bread and nothing to drink except brandy from the medicinal stores. It's surprising how you miss bread when you haven't got it. A great aching void appears in the middle of you, a sort of hole which only bread will appease. At first we tried to compensate by drinking large quantities of brandy, until finally we felt on fire and yearned for water to quench the flames.

In fact, as Jem Green might have written in his log:

Five hours out from Yarmouth. No water. No bread. Cannot understand why rats are leaving ship.

Dennis suffered most, being an habitual gourmet. In the end he said he couldn't stand it any longer, he simply had to have some coffee at least and he decided to go ashore and reconnoitre for water from a farmhouse. As he blamed Joan for not laying in fresh supplies at Yarmouth, he insisted she came with him to carry a jug and a saucepan.

They were gone a long time. We sat about, groaning with indigestion and trying not to drink the brandy, and telling one another how much we yearned for a nice cup of coffee After an hour we became anxious and peered through the gloom for them, but there was no sign and it must have been nearly midnight when they were heard crashing through the reeds.

There was something odd about them. Dennis was giggling rather stupidly as he came aboard and Joan was flashing her eyes from side to side and occasionally lowering the lids modestly. I am not a suspicious man but I would have laid ten to one that a little of the old how's-your-father had been going on out in the fields.

Beaver, however, had a mind for only one thing.

'Where's the water?' he said. 'Let's have it quickly.'

Dennis's face expressed surprise.

'Water?' he said foolishly. 'Water? We—you see there wasn't—that is we never got any.'

A positive howl of execration rent the night. I thought Arthur was going to die from sheer thirst and disappointment. Beaver was the first to recover and he demanded in a menacing fashion, 'Why isn't there any water, Dennis?'

Dennis looked like a schoolboy caught doing something wrong and actually scraped one shoe up and down his trouser leg. It was Joan who answered.

'Dennis and I are going to be married,' she said dramatically.

A further howl tore the night air, this time of surprise and disbelief. It was hardly flattering.

Harry sat back on his haunches and rocked with laughter. Arthur said 'Boyur' five times in succession and Beaver simply stared. Sheila went up and kissed them both, thus showing that she had a much nicer nature than the rest of us.

Beaver summed up his feelings thus: 'This is the end. I've seen everything this trip. Pregnant women on board, cats in the rigging, masts coming down, and now a marriage. Would anyone like to complete things by announcing that they are a reincarnation of the Venerable Bede?'

We toasted the happy pair in neat brandy, forgave them for the water and settled down to sleep. Sleep. . . . Macbeth was a chronic comatose compared with us that night. Tormented by a raging thirst, racked by stomach pains, we tossed and turned until dawn, when out of utter misery we arose and quanted along the misty river. At Stracey Arms we dashed ashore for water and relieved the worst of our worries. After that there was enough breeze to hoist sail and we made good progress to Acle Bridge.

It was ten o'clock when Acle was reached, the hour when the boat should have been delivered. Thurne Mouth was passed at eleven-thirty, and it was nearly one before *Merryweather II* and *Quiet Dawn* were quanted into Loudwater's dyke.

We had cleaned and tidied the boats under way, so we

simply unloaded our luggage in an untidy heap and made a beeline for the pub. I went to the bar to order and became aware of a tall, cadaverous individual sitting morosely on a stool at the bar, staring into space. He pushed his glass across the counter with a shaking hand and quavered, 'Another port, Bill.'

'Certainly, Mr. Loudwater,' said the barman.

I clapped the wretched boat-owner on the back.

'Cheer up, Mr. Loudwater,' I cried, with well-meant joviality. 'We've just brought *Merryweather* back safe and sound. Have a drink with us.'

Loudwater started violently.

'You from *Merryweather*?' he asked, looking at me as if I was about to knife him.

'Yes.'

'Thank 'ee. I'll have a triple port in this glass and, Bill, this gent's paying.'

I persuaded him to join us, which he did with much shaking of his head.

'You won't be using my yard next year, will you?' he begged. 'It'll ruin me. I'm giving up yachts and building only motor-cruisers with sides two inches thick. Just promise you'll never come back, will you?'

Harry bought him another triple port and he mellowed a little, regretting the decline of sail and recounting his early days on the Broads. We left him drooling over his third glass and bemoaning the fine craft he had known.

Joan and Dennis were in the pub garden as we stepped outside to go home. They were giggling and holding hands, as people will do in their circumstances.

Joan turned and waved madly at us.

'I say,' she screamed, 'wasn't it *fun*?'

National Union of Mineworkers
(NUM) 40
Nkomo, Joshua 8, 9, 10, 11, 12, 13, 15, 16–22
Nothnagel, Albert 36
Nuclear Non-Proliferation Treaty 47,
110, 126, 163, 168–169
Nyanda, Siphiwe 143
Nyerere, Julius 14, 21
Nzo, Alfred 92
Obasanjo, Olusegun 27
Odendaal, Dolf 55
Oppenheimer, Harry 35, 94
Owen, David 9, 11
PAC see Pan Africanist Congress (PAC)
Pan Africanist Congress (PAC) 4, 23,
40, 151, 153
Patriotic Front 8, 9, 15, 21
Patten, Chris 39
Pauw, Jacques 154
Pienaar, Louis 82–83, 88
Philip, Duke of Edinburgh 174
Population Registration Act 132, 133, 157
Powell, Charles 49, 71, 142
Progressive Federal Party 36, 100
Ramaphosa, Cyril 40, 166, 174–175
Reagan, Ronald 78, 84, 117
Renamo 13, 30, 32, 42, 46–47, 63, 73, 94,
150
Rhodesia 8–22, 30, 31, 42, 45, 86, 88, 167
see also Zimbabwe
Robben Island 40, 50, 63, 105, 106, 176
Roux, Jannie 63
Rowell, Anthony 167
'Rubicon' speech 27, 111
Rudolph, Piet 162
Runcie, Robert 45
Rupert, Anton 35, 58, 71
Rupert, Johann 55
SACP see South African Communist
Party (SACP)

Sampson, Anthony 102, 115, 120, 173
Sampson, Sally 115
Saunders, Stuart 35
Savimbi, Jonas 42, 78, 79, 80
Sawers, John 51
Schoeman, Renier 34
Separate Amenities Act 37, 42, 109, 133
September, Dulcie 75
Sharpeville Six 57, 59, 173
Shevardnadze, Eduard 83–84, 131
Sibiya, Khulu 104, 153
Sisulu, Albertina 40, 99, 107
Sisulu, Walter 102, 105, 106–107, 118–119,
120, 121, 123, 124, 125
Sisulu, Zwelakhe 67, 99, 123
Slovo, Joe 6, 63, 134, 143, 144, 160–161, 164
Smit, Basie 67
Smith, David 21
Smith, Ian 8, 9, 11, 15–16, 20, 21, 31
Soames, Christopher 18, 20, 21
South African Communist Party
(SACP) 4, 49, 63, 66, 107, 113, 143,
168
South West Africa People's Organisation
(Swapo) 25, 77, 79, 80, 81, 82, 88–90,
127–128, 129, 140
sports boycott 119, 157, 158, 159, 165–166
State Security Council (SSC) 54, 105
Steyn, Jan 71, 94
Steyn, Pierre 170
Steyn, Richard 144
Surtee, Yusuf 120
Suzman, Helen 1, 3, 34, 35, 36–37, 51, 52,
58–59, 60, 65, 72, 91, 95, 104, 148, 171
Swapo see South West African People's
Organisation (Swapo)
Tambo, Adelaide 120, 155
Tambo, Oliver 37, 48, 102, 115, 120, 138,
139, 140, 143, 155, 168
Thatcher, Denis 68–9